Colorful profiles of fifty of our greatest sports heroes—stars of baseball, football, basketball, track and field, golf, tennis, boxing, winter sports, swimming and sailing. From Ty Cobb to Willie Mays, from Red Grange to Joe Namath, the deeds of past and present stars are brought to life through exciting text and action-filled photographs. Every sports fan should find the stars of his favorite sport in these pages and may also meet new athletes whose excellence has put them among the greatest of this century.

GREAT
AMERICAN
ATHLETES
of the
20TH CENTURY

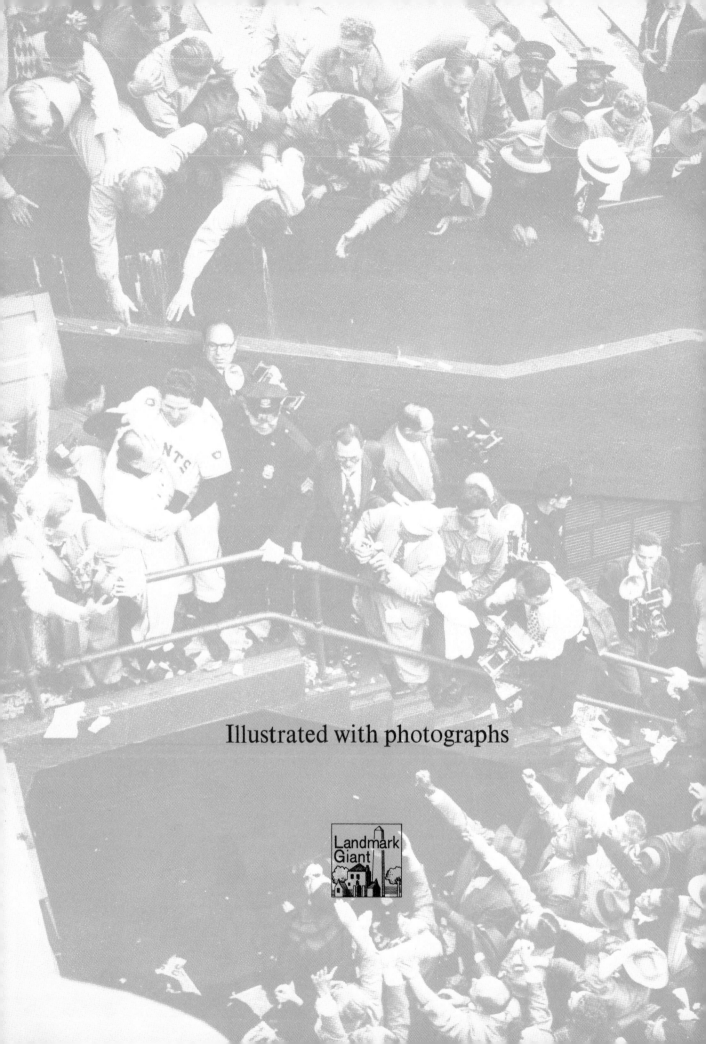

Illustrated with photographs

Landmark
Giant

GREAT

AMERICAN

ATHLETES

of the

20TH CENTURY

compiled and edited by Zander Hollander

RANDOM HOUSE NEW YORK

PHOTOGRAPH CREDITS: The Bettmann Archive, Inc., 52, 54, 60; Vernon J. Biever, viii, 125; Culver Pictures, Inc., 37, 157; Malcolm W. Emmons, i, x, 2, 3 (*both*), 4, 16, 19, 27, 70, 95, 112, 149, 151, 153; European Picture Service, 75, 140, 148, 154; New York Public Library, 59; Pictorial Parade, 30, 51, 141, 169; Ken Regan, 11, 55, 74, 92, 121; Morris Rosenfeld, 100, 102; Sy Seidman, 31, 47, 53, 138; University of California, Los Angeles, 65; United Press International, v, 5–6, 8, 13–15, 17, 21–22, 24–25, 28–29, 36, 38–40, 42, 44 (*top*), 45, 48–50, 62–64, 66, 68–69, 71, 73, 76, 77 (*bottom*), 79, 81, 84, 87–88, 90–91, 94, 99, 105, 108, 110–111, 113, 115, 117, 122 (*bottom*), 123, 126–127, 131–132, 135, 137, 139, 142, 144–145, 147, 156, 160–162, 164, 166–167; Wide World, facing false title, ii-iii, 7, 10, 18, 20, 32–33, 35, 41, 44 (*bottom*), 57, 67, 72, 77 (*top*), 83, 85, 93, 96–98, 103–104, 106, 109, 114, 116, 118–119, 122 (*top*), 128, 133, 136, 143, 152, 159, 163, 165, 168.

COVER: *top,* Malcolm W. Emmons; *middle left,* Jacino, New York *Daily News; middle right,* Arthur Rickerby, *Sports Illustrated; bottom left* and *right,* Ken Regan.

ENDPAPERS: *top left to right,* United Press International, Wide World, Malcolm W. Emmons; *bottom left to right,* Wide World, Wide World, United Press International, Wide World.

To Dad
A champ all the way

Contents

Introduction

Greatness in sport cannot be measured by cold statistics alone. Although it helps to amass a stockpile of home runs, touchdowns or trophies in whatever the sport, those who made the starting line-up in *Great American Athletes* had to present other credentials as well.

Whether stars of yesteryear or today, these men will be remembered as heroes not for athletic feats alone but because each displayed the strength of character and purpose that marks a true champion in any walk of life. Some overcame poverty; some conquered illness and physical limitations; some rose above social and racial barriers. Even the most natural athletes among them discovered early that the path to excellence is winding and unpaved.

It is hoped that these stories will serve as an inspiration to other young people who also seek the path to excellence.

Acknowledgments

This book is not the work of one writer. To provide an intimacy, variety and depth that could never have been achieved by one man, I chose a dozen authors whose writings are known to followers of sport. I am grateful to them for capturing the essence of each of the immortals in *Great American Athletes of the 20th Century*.

They are: Myron Cope; John Devaney, Fawcett Publications; Steve Gelman, *Life;* Jerry Izenberg, Newhouse Newspapers; Dan Jenkins, *Sports Illustrated;* Fred Katz, *Sport;* Tony Kornheiser, *Newsday;* John Lake; Bob McCormick; Phil Pepe, New York *Daily News;* Marty Ralbovsky, *The New York Times;* Bill Roeder, *Newsweek;* Dave Sendler, *Pageant;* the late Jack Zanger.

ZANDER HOLLANDER, EDITOR

Kareem Abdul-Jabbar

The huge electric clock was winding down, its click-click-click indicating that time was running out on the young Milwaukee Bucks. The New York Knicks were about to eliminate the Bucks from the 1970 NBA playoffs. With a sense of relief the huge capacity crowd in Madison Square Garden began a serenade.

Goodbye Lewie, goodbye Lewie,
Goodbye Lewie, we hate to see
  you go.

The solitary figure sitting on the end of the Milwaukee bench was the Bucks' rookie center Kareem Abdul-Jabbar (then known as Lew Alcindor). He pretended not to hear, and even though the Bucks had lost this season, the competitive fire still burned in him. This was one of the few times in his life that his team had lost a championship. He would one day show the Knick fans his winning ways.

Walt Frazier made a graceful apology for the Knick fans. "It was more a sigh of relief than anything else," he said. "They were glad he lost, glad to get rid of him because they know he's some kind of player."

By the time he was 12, Abdul-Jabbar stood 6-foot-8. By his 14th birthday, he stood 6–10 and he was a freshman at Power Memorial, a Catholic high school in New York. As a freshman, Abdul-Jabbar was ungainly and awkward. But he was already an intimidating force on the basketball court.

"Most big boys are awkward," said his coach, Jack Donohue, "but after his freshman year, you couldn't say that about Lewie anymore. Sure, he had talent. But others have had it and never developed it. He did

because his biggest asset was tremendous pride. I knew in his sophomore year that Lewie was going to be something special."

Others knew it, too. He was not yet halfway through high school, yet he received hundreds of letters from colleges all over the country eager for him to enroll. He even received invitations from all-white schools in the South.

It wasn't easy to overlook a seven-foot sophomore. Jabbar had grown an inch and a half since his freshman year, but that wasn't the only change in him.

Abdul-Jabbar improved quickly on the court and he learned what it's like to be seven feet tall and black. Wherever he went, people stared, giggled and pointed at him as if he were a freak. His life was far from easy. But on the basketball court, he made the game seem very easy. His height wasn't the only reason. He had grace and coordination rare in so big a man, he worked hard and he was a born competitor.

"He's a great basketball player," said Joe Lapchick, veteran coach at St. John's. "If he were 6-foot-4, he'd still be a great basketball player."

In his last three years at Power the team won 78 games and lost one, including one streak of 71 victories.

Shortly before graduation Abdul-Jabbar called a press conference at the Power Memorial gymnasium. It was May 1965 and Jabbar (still known as Lew Alcindor) was to announce the college of his choice.

"This fall I'll be attending UCLA in Los Angeles," he said. "That's the decision I came to. It has everything I want in a school."

The UCLA Bruins, had already won the

1

Kareem Abdul-Jabbar and Wilt Chamberlain start a game between Milwaukee and
Los Angeles in 1972.

NCAA championship two out of the previous three years. Fans and sportswriters
expected them to win more with their great
new center. He led his freshman team to a
21–0 record in his first year. Before he had
played one varsity game, he was selected on
pre-season All-American teams and UCLA
was voted No. 1 in pre-season polls.

The pressure was on Jabbar. People expected him to win every game and would be
surprised only if he lost. "I haven't done
anything yet," he complained. "I just want
to go out and do my thing and see if it's
good enough. You still have to go out and
win. I know one thing, the next three years
are not going to be easy."

In his sophomore year, he averaged 29.7
points a game, was named All-American
and Most Valuable Player of the NCAA
tournament. UCLA won all 30 of its games
and the national championship. In his junior year, he led UCLA to a 29–1 record
and another national championship.

In Jabbar's senior year, the Bruins lost
only one game and became the first team
ever to win three straight national championships. The experts were right, after all.
But they only made the prediction. Abdul-
Jabbar went out and did the work.

The next question was what professional
team would have the luck to get Abdul-
Jabbar. Two new teams in the NBA had
equal rights to him—Phoenix and Milwaukee. The issue was settled by the flip of a
coin. The Phoenix owner called "heads"
and lost. Abdul-Jabbar went to Milwaukee
for a reported guarantee of $1.4 million.

In one year Abdul-Jabbar took the Milwaukee Bucks from the second division to
the play-offs. The year before the Bucks had
won only 27 games. In 1969-70 they won
56. Jabbar finished second in the league in
scoring with a 28.8-point average and was
named Rookie of the Year. The Milwaukee
Bucks were on their way and even the
crowd of singers in Madison Square Garden
knew it.

The Bucks had traded with Cincinnati
for Oscar Robertson, and with two super-
stars the team dominated the league

Jabbar controls the ball for UCLA.

throughout the regular season. They set a record of 20 victories in a row and Abdul-Jabbar led the NBA in scoring with an average of 31.7 points a game.

But the play-offs represent the supreme test. With Jabbar and Robertson leading the way, Milwaukee promptly disposed of San Francisco and Los Angeles (with Wilt

Jabbar goes up for a shot and overpowers Baltimore's Wes Unseld.

Chamberlain and Jerry West) in the preliminary and semifinal series. This brought the Bucks into the championship finals against the Baltimore Bullets.

In the opening game at Milwaukee, Abdul-Jabbar gave Buck fans cause for concern. In less than three minutes he committed three personal fouls and was taken out of the game with the Bucks ahead by four points. But he returned with an 18-point third quarter and a game total of 31 points, as the Bucks won 98–88.

Jabbar and Robertson paced the Bucks to victories in games two and three (102–83, 107–99). Abdul-Jabbar shook up the Bullets with his defensive play, especially his blocking of Bullet shots. "You look up there and see the big guy up by the rim, and you just don't figure out what to do about it," complained Jack Marin of the Bullets.

Now the teams were in the fourth game, in Baltimore. And Robertson, the veteran, and Abdul-Jabbar, the second-year pro, were determined to sweep the series. Oscar

had perhaps his most brilliant night as he scored 30 and added nine assists. Jabbar was his steady self, adding 27 points and 12 rebounds. The Bucks won, 118–106. They had taken the NBA championship in four straight games. Once again Abdul-Jabbar was a champion. He received a new sports car as the outstanding player in the final series.

When his third professional season began, Jabbar announced that he had become an orthodox Muslim (not a Black Muslim) and had adopted the name Kareem Abdul-Jabbar. The man who had become famous as Lew Alcindor would now be known by his new Islamic name. If anything had changed in his basketball, it was for the better.

After watching him operate in an early-season game, Jack Ramsay, coach of the Philadelphia 76ers, came to a frightening conclusion. "Kareem Abdul-Jabbar," Ramsay said, "is a much better player than Lew Alcindor."

Jabbar relaxes after a game.

Muhammad Ali

It didn't figure to be a very long fight. Most of the Miami Beach crowd on that night in 1964 expected it to be over in a few rounds. Sonny Liston, the heavyweight champion known as "The Bear", seemed unbeatable. He had twice knocked out former champion Floyd Patterson in the first round. Now he faced a brash 22-year-old named Cassius Clay. Liston was a 10–1 favorite. Young Cassius was being thrown to the lions.

But the crowd was in for a surprise. After four rounds it was even. Clay jabbed and retreated, and Liston took the punishment and stalked his prey. Then in the fifth it seemed that the match would come to a sudden end. Clay appeared unable to come out for the bell. He blinked wildly. He couldn't see. Something was in his eyes and he wanted to quit.

Clay's trainer Angelo Dundee pushed him off the stool. "We aren't going to quit now," he said. Clay moved out for the start of the round just as referee Barney Felix was about to award the fight to Liston.

Clay jabbed and ran for a while until his eyes cleared. Then he attacked, snapping effective jabs to Liston's puffed face. He threw a powerful right that brought a roar from the crowd but missed. Then he followed up with four straight lefts to Liston's face. Liston connected with one short right to the head and the round ended.

When the bell sounded for the seventh round, it was Liston who remained on his stool. He couldn't come out for the seventh and the referee declared a technical knockout. Cassius Clay was the heavyweight champion of the world. The fans at the ringside could hardly believe it.

For months Clay (who later became

Cassius Clay (Muhammad Ali) raises his arms in triumph after knocking out Sonny Liston in 1964.

Muhammad Ali) had been telling everyone, "I am the greatest." But most people had dismissed his boasting. They should have paid more attention. The man who beat Sonny Liston was more than a loud-mouth. He had studied his craft and learned well. Blessed with lightning-fast hands and intelligence, he had beaten Liston soundly.

Cassius began his study of boxing at the age of twelve in his hometown of Louisville, Kentucky. His bicycle had been stolen. Angry about his loss, he said, "If I catch the boy who took my bike, I'll whip him good."

But to do that he had to learn how. He began taking lessons at a gym run by Patrolman Joe Martin. He learned so well that he won 180 of 184 amateur bouts. Clay fought all the way to the top of amateur boxing. His last bout was in the finals of the 1960 Olympics at Rome where he won the gold medal in the light-heavyweight class.

After his victory at Rome, Clay turned professional. He soon became a sensation both inside the ring and outside of it. He wasn't shy about his skills. He was the greatest, he said, the boxer who could "float like a butterfly, sting like a bee."

He even predicted when he would knock out his opponents. Before fighting Archie Moore he gave his prophecy in rhyme: "Archie has been livin' off the fat of the land/ I'm here to give him his pension plan/ When you come to the fight don't block aisle or door/ Cause you all goin' home after round four."

In round four, Archie Moore was counted out. The most amazing thing about Clay's predictions was that they came true.

Clay had been born Cassius Marcellus Clay. But after the fight with Liston in 1964, the new heavyweight champ announced that he had joined the Black Muslims. This religious group worshiped Allah, the god of Islam, and stressed self-help for blacks in America. Clay adopted a new Muslim name, Muhammad Ali.

Suddenly many of the fans who had cheered Ali when he defeated Sonny Liston turned against him. It didn't matter that Ali didn't smoke, drink or curse. It didn't matter that he had won his championship fair and square in the ring. It did matter that he spoke in favor of the Black Muslims, who were then thought to be dangerous and un-American. Suddenly fans weren't amused by Ali's clowning any more. Boxing looked around for a way to replace him as champion.

Ed Lassman, the president of the World Boxing Association, threatened to strip away Ali's title "because he has set a poor example for the youth of the world." But in the next three years the threat was not carried through. In that time Ali successfully defended his championship nine times.

The most famous of these defenses was against Floyd Patterson in 1965. This time, Ali was seen as the villain and Patterson was the new hero. But villain or not, Ali was the better fighter. He toyed with Patterson for 13 rounds, taunting him and punishing him. Floyd was finally declared unable to continue and Ali was the victor by a technical knockout.

In 1966 Ali was classified 1-A by his draft board. The United States was sending thousands of men to Vietnam and Ali would soon be drafted. He announced to the press that he would not serve if he were drafted.

Ali throws a punch at Floyd Patterson in defense of his title.

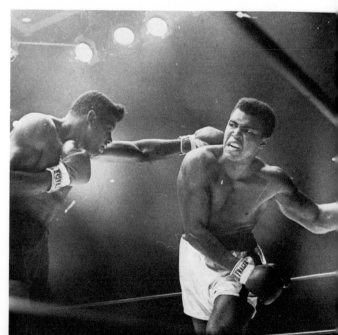

"I don't have no personal quarrel with those Viet Congs," he said.

He applied for classification as a conscientious objector on the grounds that he was a Muslim minister. The application was turned down. Other appeals to change his 1-A classification were rejected as well. Yet Ali stuck to his principles even when threatened with a jail sentence.

In March 1967 he knocked out Zora Folley in the seventh round in his ninth title defense. A month later he refused military induction in Houston. In June a Houston federal jury convicted him of draft evasion and sentenced him to five years in prison.

Ali and his lawyers appealed the court's decision and during the next four years, he was free until his case was finally decided. But boxing authorities dealt more harshly with him. He was stripped of his title and denied licenses to box by most states in the union. Jimmy Ellis, a former sparring partner of Ali, won the vacant world championship in an elimination tournament. Then in 1970 Joe Frazier defeated Ellis and was generally recognized as the world champ.

While Ali was awaiting a final decision from the Supreme Court, he spoke on college campuses, appeared on television shows and even starred in an unsuccessful Broadway musical. At the same time public opinion on the Vietnam war and on draft resistance was changing. By 1970 Ali's struggle in the courts was being recognized and supported by more and more Americans. Ali had gotten a bad deal, they said. They objected that boxing had taken away his championship long before his case in the courts had been concluded. As public opinion softened, hope rose that Ali would fight again.

In 1970 the state of Georgia granted Ali a boxing license. He signed to fight Jerry Quarry in Atlanta. Could he come back?

Kept out of the ring by boxing officials, Ali appears on television.

Three and a half years had passed since he had fought and many were skeptical. Ali defeated Quarry on a technical knockout in the third round. Then he fought Oscar Bonavena, one of the few men who had put Frazier on the canvas twice before losing a decision.

Ali fought 12 tough rounds with Bonavena, winning a decision. But Ali looked slow. He took lots of punishment and his punch combinations had lost their zip.

Still, the boxing world was impatient. They called for a championship match between Ali and Joe Frazier. Some said it would be the Fight of the Century. The big fight was finally scheduled for March 8, 1971, at Madison Square Garden in New York. Each fighter was to be paid $2,500,-000. Ali, the former champ, was unbeaten in 31 bouts. Frazier, the current champ, was unbeaten in 26. More than 20,000 people

Stunned by a punch from Joe Frazier, the new champion, Ali goes down for the first time in his pro career.

jammed the Garden to see the fight and millions more saw it on closed circuit television in the U.S. and all over the world. The whole world wanted to know who was the best heavyweight boxer: Muhammad Ali or Joe Frazier.

The fight lasted the full 15 rounds. Frazier would spend time in the hospital recovering from it, but he gave even better than he got. Joe Frazier won a unanimous 15-round decision and even knocked Ali down in the final round. Ali was no longer the greatest. Instead he was just an unsuccessful challenger.

Ali lost the fight to Frazier, but finally he won the war in the courts. On June 28, 1971, the Supreme Court, in an 8–0 decision, ruled in favor of Ali, saying in part, "It is indisputably clear . . . that the Justice Department was simply wrong as a matter of law in advising that Ali's beliefs were not religiously based and were not sincerely held."

He had always been larger than the ring he fought in. Ali's stand on his religious convictions had been upheld by the nation's highest court. But he still hadn't stopped fighting. As his court case ended, a still-confident Ali set out to win back the heavyweight crown.

Sammy Baugh

In his tight blue jeans and wide-brimmed cowboy hat he looked like an ordinary Texas ranch hand. But Sammy Baugh had never been an ordinary man, either as a football player or as a rancher.

"We sure could use a lot of rain," he said, squinting at cloudy skies in the same way he used to look downfield for a receiver. He was retired from football now and living on his ranch in the Brazos River country of West Texas.

He was soon talking football and the years rolled back as he spoke. "I enjoyed playing professional football more than college ball," he said. "The pro game is a much better game." Maybe that's why he played football for so many years and why he fought so hard to stay in the game and to succeed. Why else would his last game have ended the way it did?

Sammy Baugh was then in his sixteenth season with the Washington Redskins. His long and gaunt frame, after years of battering, looked as frail as an old picket fence. His right hand still ached from a preseason injury, and yet he was in the starting line-up for the opening game of the 1952 season. His opponents were the Chicago Cardinals and he was playing in Comiskey Park, Chicago, only a few miles from Soldiers Field, where he had begun his professional career.

Sammy was thirty-eight and far past his prime, but on this day he was superb. He danced in and out of his protective pocket as pass after pass riddled the Cardinal defense. Then an exasperated Cardinal tackle named Don Joyce, who had been tormenting Baugh all day, barreled into him again. Sammy threw with the potent right hand that had made him a football legend. But this time he was throwing a punch and it was aimed at Don Joyce. The fight lasted only long enough to get both players sent to the sidelines, banished from the game. That was the last time Sammy Baugh cocked his famous right arm on a football field.

When Baugh stalked off the field for the last time, he left behind him more than boiling tempers. He left an array of passing records that would not be surpassed for years. Some of them have never been topped. What separates Baugh from the passers that came after him is the fact that he was the original. Until he came along, the forward pass was a novelty, like a carnival sideshow, not the dynamic offensive scoring weapon that it is today. Sammy Baugh did for the forward pass what Henry Ford did for the Model-T. Others had invented the forward pass, but Baugh was the first one to make full use of it.

Sammy was born in Temple, Texas, on March 17, 1914. When he was sixteen years old, his family moved to Sweetwater, where Sam excelled on the high school basketball, football and baseball teams.

When he wasn't playing in a game, he was busy practicing. One of his favorite pastimes was firing a football through the middle of an old automobile tire that was hung from a tree branch with a piece of rope. When he was satisfied that he could throw at a stationary target without missing, he began swinging the tire and throwing at it while running to his right or left.

At first, he was an end on the high school team. But one day his coach noticed the way Sammy threw the ball back after he had gone downfield for a pass. "You're a tailback now," the coach proceeded to inform him. He was a pretty good one, too, but scouts for the major college teams didn't seem to notice. When he graduated, Sammy still hadn't decided whether to go to college or seek a baseball career. But one day, when he was playing third base for a sandlot baseball team in Abilene, he caught the eye of Leo "Dutch" Meyer, the head baseball and freshman football coach at Texas Christian University.

Through Meyer's recommendation, Sammy received a baseball scholarship at TCU. Meyer knew all about Baugh's great arm, and when he became varsity football coach a year later, he encouraged Sammy to develop other football skills.

In his junior year, Sammy led TCU to the Southwest Conference Championship and a Sugar Bowl meeting with LSU on New Year's Day. On the day of the Sugar Bowl, the field was soggy from heavy rains. Footing in the mud and slime was unsteady and it was difficult to get a good grip on the ball. Yet Sam made the difference between the two teams with his tremendous punts; TCU won the game, 3–2. As a

As quarterback for Texas Christian in 1936, Sam was the finest college player in the country.

senior in 1936, Sammy blended all his great natural talents into a spectacular season. He passed, ran and punted TCU to victory over one opponent after another. And he did it with such regularity that, one day, TCU center Ki Aldrich looked across the line of scrimmage at an opposing Texas team and announced, "Gentlemen, Mr. Baugh is going to pass again. I don't know just where it will go, but it'll be good. Be ready." Baugh did pass and it was completed.

Sammy's crowning achievement as a college player came in his last regular-season game, when he masterminded a 9–0 victory over unbeaten and untied Santa Clara in the football upset of the year. Then he completed his career at Texas Christian by leading the Horned Frogs to a 16–6 win over Marquette in the Cotton Bowl. Sam made most All-America teams that year, but he failed to convince a majority of the experts that a good college passer had any value in professional football.

George Preston Marshall, owner of the Washington Redskins, was able to draft Baugh after all the other teams had had their pick of college players. Nobody else seemed interested, not even Baugh himself. Sammy still was aiming for a career in baseball, since he felt that he wouldn't last more than two or three years in pro football. Marshall, however, made him a tempting proposition: "Play for me this fall for the highest pay check a player ever got, plus a bonus for signing. Then, if you want, you can try baseball next spring. After that, you can make up your own mind."

The Redskin coach, Ray Flaherty, did not share his boss's enthusiasm for the new passing wizard. When Baugh walked onto the field for his first practice session, Flaherty challenged him immediately: "They tell me you're quite a passer."

"I reckon I can throw a little," Sammy answered.

"Show me," said Flaherty. "Hit that receiver in the eye."

"Which eye?" asked Baugh.

In his rookie year, Sammy guided the Redskins to an Eastern Division crown with an 8–3 record. Then, in the championship game against the imposing Chicago Bears, he led a deadly passing attack. In the second half he threw three touchdown passes, covering 55, 78 and 33 yards. The Redskins won, 28–21. Sammy's football career was secure.

In the spring of 1938, Sammy failed to make the St. Louis Cardinals baseball team. This finally convinced him to pour all his energy and devotion into football. For the next fifteen years, Sammy threw more passes than anyone had thought possible. He helped the Redskins win four more divisional titles and another championship, while setting nearly every passing record in the book. Most of the records have been beaten now by such illustrious successors as Sid Luckman, Bobby Layne, Y. A. Tittle and Johnny Unitas. But his personal statistics are still remarkable, especially since he was the first of the great passers. Sammy attempted 2,995 passes and completed 1,693, for a total of 22,085 yards and 186 touchdowns.

Sammy set another record by playing in the National Football League for sixteen seasons. He is the first regular offensive player to have played that long.

Slingin' Sam outlasted several young Redskin quarterbacks who were hoping to replace him, too. Sports writers were naming his replacement years before he retired. But Sammy lasted longer in the NFL than most of his challengers.

On occasion, he has come out of retirement to try his hand at coaching. He coached at Hardin–Simmons University for several years. Then he became head coach of the New York Titans (now the Jets) and the Houston Oilers of the American Football League. In January of 1966, Sam again responded to the call of football to become a backfield coach for the Detroit Lions.

Sammy Baugh is a tough man but an honest one. Perhaps he made his most succinctly honest statement after the Redskins had been slaughtered 73–0, by the Chicago Bears in the 1940 NFL Championship game. Someone asked Sam if the game might have been different if a Redskin end had hung onto one of his first-quarter passes.

"Yeah," Sammy answered. "That would have made it 73–6."

Baugh is seen here as the head coach of the New York Titans. He became backfield coach of the Detroit Lions in 1966.

Doc Blanchard and Glenn Davis

Glenn Davis was eager to get back to the United States Military Academy, even though he knew the toughest ordeal of his life awaited him there. He would have to wear a uniform, snap to attention hundreds of times a day, and march for miles in the early morning while his body and mind were weary from lack of sleep. Since the Military Academy combined college instruction with Army training, he would return from the early morning marches to spend hours in classrooms each day. Then he would study until he fell asleep at his desk with his books still open in front of him.

Glenn knew, too, that he would play football at the Academy. On the train from his home in California to the Academy in West Point, New York, he sat next to a man named Clark Shaughnessy. Shaughnessy had once coached the football team at Stanford University, and he told Davis he knew of another boy who would be playing football at West Point in the 1944 season. "The boy's going to be a great back," Shaughnessy said. "I know you'll meet him. His name is Blanchard. Felix Blanchard."

A few weeks later Davis met Blanchard at football practice. They did not know then that soon people would be unable to think of one of them without thinking of the other as well. Nor did they know that they had something very important in common: each had a special reason for wanting to succeed at West Point.

Davis wanted to succeed at West Point because he had failed there the previous year. Along with his twin brother, Ralph, Glenn had entered the Academy in 1943. The overwhelming work had defeated him.

Though he had studied each night until he was exhausted and had arisen each morning at 4:00 A.M. to study some more, he had failed math and flunked out of the Academy. Since then he had taken a cram course in math at Pomona College in California, where he had done well enough to get another chance at West Point. He was determined not to fail again.

Blanchard had a different reason for wanting to succeed. All his life he and his father had been very close. In Bishopville, South Carolina, people had always called his father "Big Doc" and him "Little Doc." Big Doc, a physician, loved football and had encouraged his son to learn the game before he was old enough to go to school. Big Doc had played football at St. Stanislaus Prep School in Mississippi and he sent Little Doc there to play, too. After prep school Little Doc went on to the University of North Carolina. But by 1942 the United States was fighting in World War II, so Little Doc enlisted as a private in the Army. Meanwhile, Big Doc worked night and day to get his son admitted to West Point.

In the fall of 1944, Little Doc entered the Academy to study for his college degree and his army officer's commission. But now he was just called Doc. His father had died and young Doc Blanchard was determined to make good use of the chance his father had gotten him.

Through their first months together at West Point, Blanchard and Davis did well in the classroom and spectacularly well on the football field. After Army had played and won a few games that season, it was obvious that no two backfield men had ever worked so well together as Blanchard and Davis. Davis was the halfback, the man of speed. Blanchard was the fullback, the man of power. The only way an opponent could throttle Doc's power was to pack the middle of the line. But with the defenses jammed in tight to stop Doc, Glenn would run around the ends for long gains. If the defensive line loosened up to catch Glenn, Doc would rocket through the middle for first downs and touchdowns. Soon sports writers and football fans were calling Davis "Mr. Outside" and Blanchard "Mr. Inside."

After Army walloped Notre Dame in 1944, the Notre Dame coach, Ed McKeever, sent the following wire home: "Have just seen Superman in the flesh. He wears No. 35 on his Army jersey. His name is Felix 'Doc' Blanchard."

If Doc, with a height of 6 feet, 1½ inches and a weight of 200 pounds, was Superman, Glenn, at 5 feet, 10 inches tall and 173 pounds, was at least Superboy. In the 1944 season, Doc scored nine touchdowns and averaged 7.1 yards per carry. Glenn led the nation in scoring with twenty touchdowns, and gained an average of 12.4 yards per carry. Army won every game it played, achieving its first perfect record since 1916.

The big game for Army in the 1945 season was the one against Navy. Army was the number one college team in the country and Navy was number two. World War II had just ended and thousands of Americans felt a special interest in the service academies. In addition, thousands of men were still in the services and listened to the Army–Navy game by shortwave radio in all parts of the world.

In the game, Mr. Outside scored two touchdowns and Mr. Inside scored three. Army won, 32–13, its eighteenth straight

Army coach Red Blaik (left) relaxes with his backfield stars Doc Blanchard (center) and Glenn Davis (right).

victory. It was the biggest victory yet for Blanchard and Davis.

Doc Blanchard was indeed living up to the high goals his father had set for him. Not only was he a star football player, but he was a fine student and award-winning soldier as well. He had even been picked to serve on the guard of honor at President Franklin Roosevelt's funeral in 1945.

Glenn, meanwhile, was fulfilling the goals

he had set for himself. He was doing well in the classroom and, though he didn't like military life as much as Doc did, he was a good soldier. He was also the best all-round athlete in the history of West Point. He starred for the track team and he was such a fine baseball player that one day he would be offered—and would turn down—a fabulous major league contract.

Doc was the better soldier and Glenn

Glenn Davis heads for the second touchdown of the 1945 Army-Notre Dame game. Final score: Army 48, Notre Dame 0.

the better athlete, but they were different in other ways, too. "I was a worrier," Glenn recalled years later. "I worried about my studies and I worried about games. Everybody knew it, too. I couldn't keep my emotions to myself. Doc took everything in stride. About the only time anyone knew he was worked up about something was when he talked or kicked in his sleep."

Doc's roommates reported that he often talked in his sleep the night before a game. "There he goes," he would yell. "Tackle him. Get him." But at other times he was a soft-spoken, joking, easy-going fellow. His best friend at the Academy was Glenn's twin brother, Ralph. "They're like a couple of puppies," an Army instructor once said. "Always foolin' and wrasslin' around."

Doc never fooled around on the football field, of course. In 1945, he won the Heisman Trophy, which is awarded annually to the best player in college football. Then he helped Army to another undefeated season in 1946. Glenn won the 1946 Heisman Trophy.

Blanchard and Davis graduated from West Point in June, 1946, and entered the Army as second lieutenants. Glenn left military service in 1950 and played a few years of professional football with the Los Angeles Rams. Doc remained in the Army.

But despite their success in other fields, Doc Blanchard and Glenn Davis will be remembered by sports fans as the finest backfield combination that football has ever seen—Mr. Inside and Mr. Outside.

Blanchard snags a pass from Davis in the 1946 contest with undefeated Notre Dame. The battle ended in a scoreless tie.

Bill Bradley

The food was steaming hot, the table was set and the Bradleys were about to sit down to dinner. But someone was missing: the Bradleys' teenage son, Bill.

Mrs. Bradley wasn't worried. This wasn't the first time Bill had been late for dinner and she knew exactly where to find him. Although high-school basketball practice had ended hours earlier, she knew Bill would still be out on the court, practicing alone. He would be so absorbed in his work

that he would remain there until she drove to school to remind him that dinner was on the table.

Bill never meant to keep the others waiting; he was usually considerate and polite. But he was also fiercely competitive and determined to succeed at whatever he did. He believed that hard work led to success. Ed Macauley, the old college and professional basketball star, had once told Bill: "You always have to give a hundred percent because if you don't, someone, someplace, *will* give a hundred percent and will beat you when you meet." Bill never forgot Macauley's advice.

In Crystal City, Missouri, where he was born on July 28, 1943, people were proud of Bill. He was an honor student, an Eagle Scout and a basketball star. He was also one of the boys. He enjoyed parties and at bull sessions he was a good listener and a good talker.

Bill was self-confident. He wasn't afraid of being called a sissy or teacher's pet. He did what he thought was right. "As long as I can make a paper better or try for a better grade," he said, "I'm going to do it. The extra effort is something I owe myself. It helps me understand a subject better, and it helps me better myself."

Those who knew him were impressed with Bill's ability to do so well in so many areas. They wondered, however, if he would be able to keep up the pace when he entered college, where the schoolwork and the athletic competition would be much tougher.

Bill wondered about it, too, as he entered Princeton University in 1961. "I had the

Bill Bradley shoots from the foul line.

16

natural doubts and fears of an 18-year-old boy traveling 1,200 miles from a high school of 400 to attend a college of 3,000. I wondered if I could make it athletically and academically."

It was important for Bill to find an expression of spiritual interest, too. During his high-school years he had joined the Fellowship of Christian Athletes, an organization of sports stars dedicated to the Christian life. He was determined to continue his Fellowship work at Princeton.

Bill soon discovered that in order to do all the things he wanted, and to do them well, he would have to sacrifice leisure time and work hard even when exhausted. He attended classes three or four hours a day and studied an average of seven hours each weekday, twelve to fourteen hours on Saturday and, often, ten hours on Sunday. He practiced basketball four hours a day, an hour more than anyone else on the team. And he made speeches at churches and attended camps and clinics of the Fellowship of Christian Athletes.

People around the country began getting interested in Bill's hectic life at Princeton when he made the All-America basketball team in his sophomore year. They became even more interested when he became an All-America again as a junior and proved that he was probably the best college basketball player in the nation.

Bill played backcourt and forward. He scored on jump shots and hook shots, driving shots and set shots. He fed pass after pass to his teammates for layups, prompting people to say that he didn't shoot enough himself. Further, he was uncanny at crucial moments. When Princeton desperately needed a field goal, a rebound or miraculous defensive play to win the game, Bradley inevitably made it. When Princeton desperately needed a rebound, Bradley with

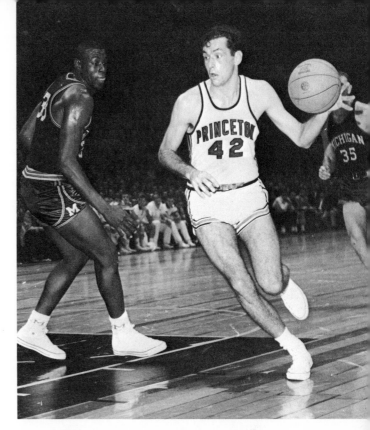

Dribbling around his Michigan opponent in the Holiday Festival tournament, Bradley heads for the basket.

his 6-foot, 5-inch, 205-pound frame would leap up among taller, heavier, stronger opponents and pull the ball off the backboards. When Princeton desperately needed a miraculous defensive play, Bradley made that, too. He led Princeton to upset after upset over schools more prominent in basketball.

Terry Dischinger, the Purdue University basketball All-America, had once met Bill and said, "As a ballplayer, he's great. But I'm more impressed with him as a person. He's the kind of guy you like to know. The kind you like to have as a friend."

Bradley played in the United States Olympic basketball trials, and was selected to the squad. He became the number one star as the United States won the Olympic gold medal in Tokyo. Bill returned to the United States, began writing his Princeton senior thesis on Harry Truman's 1940 senatorial campaign and continued playing

17

collegiate basketball. In the Holiday Festival Tournament, Princeton played the nation's top-ranked team, Michigan, in the final round. Bradley scored 41 points and almost single-handedly gave Princeton a 75–63 lead with his sensational passing, defense and rebounding. With 4:37 left to play, he fouled out and Princeton lost, 80–78.

Princeton won the Ivy League title, then advanced to the semifinals of the National Collegiate Athletic Association tournament, the farthest any Ivy League team had ever gone. In the semifinals, Bradley was outstanding again, but again Princeton was beaten by Michigan.

Bradley's last game with Princeton was against Wichita for third place in the NCAA tournament. In the first half he scored nineteen points. During the second half, Princeton called time out. His teammates told Bill that they wanted to help him win the tournament scoring record by feeding him the ball every time they gained possession.

Leading Princeton to victory, Bradley set not one record but two. Dropping in his hooks, jump shots, layups and turn shots, he totaled 58 points, the most ever scored in an NCAA tournament game. He had also scored 177 points in the tournament, another record.

Bradley was picked as the first choice of the New York Knickerbockers, one of the highest honors a college player can achieve. He was also awarded a Rhodes scholarship, one of the highest honors a college student can receive. He decided to continue his studies at Oxford University in England and it wasn't until 1967 that he returned to the United States to play basketball. He had something to prove: that he could make it as a professional.

He signed a four-year contract for a reported $400,000 with the Knicks and joined them midway through the 1967-68 season. It wasn't long before he showed that he could be a team leader in the National Basketball Association just as he had been on the court at Princeton. Two years after Bill became a Knick, the team won its first NBA championship. Bill Bradley had proved he could make it as a professional.

Knick Star Bill Bradley drives around teammate Willis Reed toward the basket.

Jimmy Brown

When Jimmy Brown was a teenager, he received a letter from Casey Stengel, then the manager of the New York Yankees. Brown had been pitching no-hitters and slugging home runs for his high-school team, and Stengel wondered if Jimmy would be interested in playing for the Yankee organization. "I don't think so," Jimmy told his friends. "There's not enough action in baseball."

If it was action Jimmy craved, a Syracuse boxing promoter had the answer. Shortly after Jimmy graduated from college, the promoter offered him $150,000 to sign a three-year contract as a prize fighter. "He's 6-foot-2, weighs 225 pounds and is fast on his feet," said Marv Jensen, manager of former middleweight champion Gene Fullmer. "He's got all the basics to become the heavyweight champ."

Everyone, it seemed, wanted Jimmy Brown. He was perhaps the finest all-round athlete since Jim Thorpe. As a high-school senior he averaged 38 points a game in basketball. In college he once won the high jump at a track meet while warming up for a lacrosse game. In lacrosse he was All-America. In golf he quickly began shooting in the 70s—without a single lesson.

Despite his versatility, Jimmy had no difficulty in deciding on his athletic future. Football had always been his favorite sport because it provided the perfect action-filled showcase for his speed, power and intelligence. When the Cleveland Browns of the National Football League drafted him Number One following the 1956 college football season, Jimmy signed eagerly. His signature marked the start of the pro career of the greatest ball-carrier in history.

Jim Brown has been compared to such football greats as Bronko Nagurski and Jim Thorpe.

The NFL record book is liberally sprinkled with Brown's achievements over an unmatched nine-year period through 1965. He was the only player whose rushing yardage in a single season totaled more than a mile (1,863 yards in 1963). He registered four of the best ground-gaining games in NFL history, twice hitting a mark of 237 yards. In addition, he gained over a thousand yards in each of seven seasons and led in rushing for eight of his nine playing years. When he finished, he owned NFL career records for the most touchdowns (126 on runs and

19

pass receptions) and for the most touchdowns scored by rushing (106).

With Brown's records came tangible rewards. He was the highest salaried running back in history and he became a successful businessman in the off-season. When he retired from football in 1966, he turned his talents to movie acting and to a role in the affairs of heavyweight boxing champion Cassius Clay.

Life has been good to Jimmy, and yet he has known sadness and frustration as well. His friend Ernie Davis, who had broken some of Jimmy's records at Syracuse University and who seemed set to join Jimmy in the Cleveland backfield, died of leukemia before ever playing pro football. Jimmy has also had to pay a physical price for his own success. Elbows have been flailed across his mouth, fists have clubbed his throat. There have been games when

he was so dazed he couldn't remember his play. Today he has an elbow that periodically must be drained of water, and his hands are slashed with scars.

In some ways these discordant notes are reminiscent of Jimmy's earlier days; life has seldom been easy for him. He was born on February 17, 1936, on St. Simon's Island, Georgia. When he was two his parents separated. For five years he lived with his great-grandmother while his mother went north to work as a maid. He rejoined his mother when he was seven, in Manhasset, New York.

Jimmy's enormous strength became apparent while he was still in high school. As a senior he averaged 14.9 yards a carry in football and was feared as a defensive linebacker. In the final game of the season Manhasset High's unbeaten record appeared to be in danger. Garden City, trailing by a point, began rolling toward a touchdown. In the last eleven plays of the game, Jimmy made seven tackles. He stopped Garden City, giving Manhasset its first undefeated team in twenty-nine years.

Sought by forty-five colleges, Jimmy chose Syracuse, even though the school refused to give him a scholarship until he had proved himself on the freshman football team. This didn't take him long and he developed a big reputation in basketball, track and field and lacrosse as well. But football was Jimmy's sport. By his senior year he was being called "the East's most powerful running back since Army's Doc Blanchard." He scored 14 touchdowns and 22 extra points that season and made most All-America teams. In the last regular

Brown shakes off a Giant tackler on his way to a touchdown during the 1965 season.

20

Two Texas Christian tacklers combine to stop Brown during the 1957 Cotton Bowl Game after he has returned a kickoff 26 yards.

season game of 1956, Brown rolled up 43 points against Colgate. Then he scored 21 more in a heartbreaking 28–27 defeat to Texas Christian in the Cotton Bowl.

Jimmy was selected to the College All-Star team, which he considered a great honor. But he was bitterly disappointed when he saw little action in the game against the defending pro champions, the New York Giants. Brown was so disgusted that he skipped the team party and drove all night to the Cleveland training camp. He played in the team's second exhibition game and on one draw play ran 48 yards for a touchdown. After the run, coach Paul Brown called Jimmy over. "You're my fullback," the coach announced.

Jimmy's rookie season was spotty at times, but in the ninth game he put on a demonstration that accurately foretold his future. Against Los Angeles he scored four times and gained 237 yards, the greatest

running performance in NFL annals. Cleveland went on to win the Eastern Conference championship before being mauled by Detroit, 59–14, in the title game.

Jimmy continued to dominate all other ball-carriers season after season, but dissension was beginning to build up on the Cleveland team. The players were unhappy about the lack of communication between them and Coach Paul Brown. Jimmy was also being used more often than ever before. In one game he carried thirty-four times. "Aren't thirty-four carries too many?" someone asked him. "Can't it shorten your career?"

"If the coach says carry fifty times, then I carry fifty times," said Jim.

In 1962 the multiple problems reached the exploding point. For the first time since his rookie season, Jimmy gained fewer than a thousand yards. But after the end of the season, Blanton Collier was named to re-

21

place Paul Brown as coach. With Jimmy gaining more than a mile in 1963, the Browns started building momentum. In 1964 it was apparent that they were a championship threat. They had developed a diversified attack that took some of the pressure off Jimmy.

At midseason the Browns won a crucial game with Pittsburgh and Jimmy, playing with a badly injured toe, went over the 10,000-yard mark for his career. It was one of his greatest accomplishments. But it would have meant little to Brown if his team hadn't won the Eastern Conference title. In the championship game, they defeated Baltimore 27–0 to become the NFL champions.

"I've had a lot of individual glory," said Jimmy at the season's end. "But individual glory doesn't mean too much to me. If you play long enough you'll set a lot of records. A man can play a lifetime and set a lot of records and never win a championship. James Brown is only one-fortieth of an organization. The championship is really what I've needed, and what I've wanted."

Brown carrying, protected by an over-zealous blocker during the 1964 title game against Baltimore.

Dick Button

When Dick Button was five years old, he proudly announced that he had already decided his future. "I'm going to be either a priest or a figure skater."

People congratulated him on his decision, but reminded him that there was one slight problem. "Only Catholic boys can become priests," they said, "and you're not a Catholic."

"If I can't be a priest," he replied, "then I guess I'll just *have* to be a skater."

But Dick's figure-skating career appeared to be as ill-fated as his desire to be a priest. When he was eleven, he still hadn't had any formal training and he wasn't much better than dozens of other kids who skated on the local pond. One day he lugged his old skates up to a country club near his home in Englewood, New Jersey, and watched a group of youngsters taking lessons. For weeks after that, he tried to imitate the things they were doing.

His father had no trouble picking out Dick's present that Christmas. But when Dick unwrapped his pair of gleaming new skates, he was obviously disappointed. Mrs. Button took her husband aside and explained the problem. "You bought hockey skates," she said. "Dick had his heart set on figure skates."

At first, Dick's father thought that figure skating was sissy stuff. But he exchanged the skates and by the end of that winter he was as enthusiastic about Dick's skating as Dick himself. The only problem was that Dick's instructor didn't share this enthusiasm. When his father asked about further lessons for Dick, she told him that Dick could never expect to be a great skater.

Grace is fundamental to skating, and all the instructor could see in Dick was a five-foot, two-inch, 160-pound butterball whose movements on the ice were anything but graceful. But her appraisal only made Dick's father angry. Soon afterward he asked famed skating coach Gus Lussi to take a look at Dick. Lussi agreed that the boy might have possibilities and arranged to coach him. Dick quickly began to improve under Lussi's unyielding demands for perfection.

Sometimes the lessons were painful. One day Lussi became annoyed when Dick constantly forgot to point his toe. In his slight accent, the coach said to Dick: "What does a streetcar conductor do when he goes around a corner?" Dick shook his head.

"To warn pedestrians," said Lussi, "he stamps on the foot bell." And with that, the coach lifted his skate and stamped across the toe of Dick's skating boot. Dick howled in pain—but never again did he forget about pointing his toe.

In April, 1943, Dick entered his first tournament and finished second in the Eastern novice event. To Dick, this was not a satisfactory start. "I want to win, not place second," he said. "And I can do it."

He kept up a rigorous training schedule that began at 5:30 each morning and spent five or six hours a day on the ice. His boyish layers of fat became muscle and he soon attained his adult proportions of 5-feet-10, 175 pounds.

In 1944, at the age of fourteen, Dick won the men's national novice championship and the next year he won the junior championship.

In an amazingly short time he had gone from an ice-skating eyesore to a fellow with true Olympic potential. He won his first senior men's title in 1946 when he was sixteen and the following year he made his

Against a background of snow-covered Alps, Dick Button glides to a figure-skating gold medal in the 1948 Olympics.

mark in international competition, finishing a surprising second at the world championships. By 1948 he was more than ready for the Olympics in St. Moritz, Switzerland. He warmed up for the big moment by winning the European title.

When he prepared to take the ice at St. Moritz, Dick seemed much more at ease than either of his parents. His mother could scarcely hold on to her pencil and his father repeatedly dropped his cigar. But they had nothing to worry about. In the first half of the competition—the compulsory figures—Dick was superb. He performed each of the five maneuvers exactly as Gus Lussi had taught him. Dick piled up a commanding lead, and his strong point —free skating—was still to come. In his five-minute routine set to music, Dick flawlessly performed spins and jumps that no one else would even attempt. It was an historic victory both for Dick and for the United States. He was the first American figure skater to win an Olympic gold medal.

He then entered the world championships and won them, too. For his performance in 1948, Dick was named amateur athlete of the year.

Everywhere Dick went after his triumph he was asked if he would turn professional. He patiently explained that he wanted to go on to college and doubted that he would ever skate for money. He enrolled at Harvard, majoring in business. People wondered whether he would find the time to maintain his difficult studies and still practice the several hours a day necessary to maintain his skating form. A less determined fellow might not have, but Dick refused to throw away all he had achieved. He won the next four United States and world championships, studying between whirls on the ice.

At the 1952 Olympics in Oslo, Norway, he caused a controversy when he insisted on staying in a private hotel room rather than at the Olympic dormitory. Harvard officials had permitted Dick to miss classes

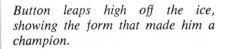

Button leaps high off the ice, showing the form that made him a champion.

Button displays flashing skates in his defense of the Olympic championship in 1952.

only if he promised to keep up with his work while he was away, and Button felt he needed the privacy of his own room. He was called a softie and a snob. But the name-calling was forgotten when he easily skated to his second gold medal.

It seemed that Dick Button could go on winning gold medals and amateur championships for years. But after his graduation from Harvard, he was faced with earning a living, so he turned professional. In late 1952, he became the star of Ice Capades and in the years that followed he organized and skated in his own ice shows. In 1959 he took his troupe to the Soviet Union as part of a cultural exchange program and

his efforts to help melt the cold war were widely praised.

Dick Button will always be remembered as one of the most glamorous figures in sports history. As an amateur he won seven straight U. S. titles, five straight world championships and two Olympic gold medals. But to Dick the glamor always looked pale compared with the thousands of hours of hard work it took to make him a champion. He frequently thought back to the night when an instructor had casually dismissed his chances of ever being a great skater. It wasn't that the instructor didn't know skating. She just didn't know Dick Button.

25

Wilt Chamberlain

Alex Hannum had left coaching to become a building contractor. When the owner of the San Francisco Warriors of the National Basketball Association asked him to take over the club, Hannum's thoughts immediately centered on one San Francisco player: Wilt Chamberlain. Wilt had a talent that every coach dreams of. Yet there was the danger that he could wreck all Hannum's coaching efforts.

"Does Chamberlain demand to play the full forty-eight minutes of every game?" Hannum asked.

"Absolutely not," replied club owner Eddie Gottlieb.

"Is Chamberlain going after points to ensure his high salary?"

"Absolutely not."

"Okay," said Hannum. "You've got yourself a coach."

Ever since Wilt Chamberlain began playing basketball for the University of Kansas, he has provoked doubts such as Hannum's. On a given night Wilt can play basketball better than anyone alive. And yet he has seldom been on a winning team. This contradiction is the center of Wilt's story.

Seven-feet, one-inch tall and weighing 290 pounds, Chamberlain has revolutionized basketball. He has shown that a big man need not be slow or clumsy and that a good big man is almost impossible to stop. Wilt's talent is so great that he is expected to produce championships almost single-handedly. And yet, when his team loses, he is accused of being a ball-hog and a poor team player. He averages nearly 35 points per game and once scored 100 in a single contest. Yet he has been labeled uncoachable, lazy and selfish.

Throughout his career, the label that stung him the most, however, was "loser."

Wilt used to reply to his critics: "Take Jimmy Brown in football. Jimmy played *seven* years before he was on a winner. Did people call him a loser?"

But Wilt doesn't have to answer anyone nowadays. On April 24, 1967, Wilt became a winner! On that night he led the Philadelphia 76ers to the championship of the NBA. And Wilt stopped being a loser.

When Wilt was a boy, no one would even have expected him to be a basketball player. He was born in Philadelphia on August 21, 1936. At first, he had no reason to expect that he would be extremely tall. His father and mother were both less than six feet and the tallest of his brothers was only six feet, four inches. In seventh grade he began to play basketball. Although he was better than most boys his age, there was still no sign of great height or ability. Then, when he was fifteen, he grew four inches in three months. By the time he entered Overbrook High School, he was six feet eleven, and had begun to attract attention.

Chamberlain was not a loser at Overbrook High. His teams won the All-Public title three years in a row and the All-City championship two years out of three. He acquired the nicknames "Wilt the Stilt" and the "Big Dipper" and soon two hundred colleges were competing for him. He was in such demand that government tax men, suspicious that some colleges would be offering him money under the table, kept an eye on him even in high school. Still in his teens, he had become almost a legend.

Wilt's 76ers won the NBA Eastern Division championship in 1966, but lost to the Celtics in the second round of the play-offs.

At the University of Kansas, where he finally enrolled, it was taken for granted that he would carry the Kansas team to the national championship. In his sophomore year, he almost did. But in the final game of the NCAA tournament Kansas lost to North Carolina by one point in three overtimes. North Carolina coach Frank McGuire assigned two, three and sometimes even four men to cover Wilt and he was held to 23 points. That was as close as Wilt ever got to a college championship. The next year Kansas didn't make the finals.

Wilt found in his second varsity year that Kansas opponents were so determined to stop him that playing basketball was no longer fun. "Coaches began to pile *four* men on me and leave one guy to cover the rest of the Kansas team," he recalls. "I was guarded so closely that I thought I was going to spend the rest of my life looking out at the world through wiggling fingers, forearms and elbows." Another favorite trick of Kansas opponents was to freeze the ball on the theory that, if Wilt couldn't get the ball, he couldn't score.

Wilt left Kansas and became a professional after his junior year. He played first for the Harlem Globetrotters and then moved to the Philadelphia Warriors in the NBA. The Warriors were in financial trouble and Wilt's teammates resented being

stagehands for Chamberlain's act. The team was soon transferred to San Francisco and Alec Hannum became head coach.

Although Hannum had originally been wary of coaching Wilt, he was the man who finally brought about the biggest change in the "Big Dipper." He soon transformed Wilt from a high-scoring showman to a team player who would also set up shots for his teammates and use his tremendous advantage on defense. But the talent-poor Warriors failed and early in 1965 Wilt was traded to the new Philadelphia team, the 76ers. There Wilt led his team in hot pursuit of the Boston Celtics, whose superiority in the NBA had not been challenged for years. In the 1965-66 season the 76ers, with Wilt having his finest all-around campaign, made their boldest bid to overtake the Celtics. They reached the playoffs and many thought that Wilt and his gang would finally end the Celtics dynasty. But the 76ers simply weren't up to the task.

The "loser" label was still fixed on Wilt after that, but NBA players began to warm to him and they admitted privately that Wilt had accomplished more wonders than anyone had a right to expect. In January, 1966, he broke the all-time NBA scoring record, adding it to his long list of other records in scoring and rebounding. Despite his critics, Wilt has already rewritten the record books of professional basketball.

Since Wilt broke into the NBA, club owners have passed several new rules to keep the tall men like Wilt from gaining too great an advantage. They have widened the free-throw lane by two feet, outlawed the out-of-bounds pass over the backboards

His tremendous size and agility made it possible for Wilt to overpower his college opponents.

28

and stiffened interpretations of goal-tending. It is now against the rules to guide in a teammate's shot or to take a lob pass at basket height and stuff the ball through. But despite the rules changes, Chamberlain was able to show he could be a winner, leading the 76ers to a 68–13 regular-season record and then play-off victories over perennial champion Boston and finally over his old team, San Francisco, for the NBA crown.

Philadelphia's reign lasted only one season, however, and Chamberlain's critics began to grumble again. He was traded to Los Angeles and there he changed his role from super scorer to super feeder on a team whose best shooter was Jerry West.

Wilt has often complained about his critics, his rough opponents and those who stare at him on the street as if he were a freak. But gradually his irritation with the world has mellowed and the world's irritation with him has softened, too. His critics have become less outspoken, his opponents have watched him score despite injuries and Wilt has learned to handle the gawkers without becoming angry.

If some of his irritation remains, it is because big men never attract the fans who root for the underdog. As Wilt says, "Everybody pulls for David, nobody roots for Goliath."

As a Laker, Wilt keeps the ball from the New York Knicks.

Ty Cobb

It was a late-season game in 1910 and Ty Cobb of the Detroit Tigers was dashing toward third base. He hit the dirt, his razor-sharp spikes high in the air. Suddenly there was a cry of pain from Frank "Home Run" Baker, the Philadelphia Athletics' third baseman. Baker held his arm in agony and blood from a deep gash oozed through his fingers. Ty Cobb, baseball's most feared man, had struck again.

Cobb demonstrates the high slide that terrified opposing infielders.

Cobb was to live for fifty-one more years and would always insist he never spiked Baker intentionally. But on that September day in 1910, with the A's battling for the American League pennant, not a single fan in the Philadelphia ball park was willing to believe in Cobb's innocence. Only the alert umpires and ushers kept Cobb from being mauled by the crowd.

A few days later Cobb received a letter. "If you play against Philadelphia again," the note read, "you will be shot."

Cobb was scared, but only to a point. The next time the Tigers came to Philadelphia, Cobb was in his usual spot in the outfield. Only once did he show any fright. In the seventh inning a car backfired behind the ball park and teammate Sam Crawford swore Cobb jumped at least a foot. But no one took any shots at Cobb that day. He had called the letter writer's bluff.

Few men in sports ever have been as widely disliked as Cobb. Yet even his fiercest enemies had to concede that he had two virtues: courage and amazing baseball ability. Both qualities were shown in one particular series witnessed by legendary sports writer Grantland Rice. "Each of Cobb's legs was a mass of raw flesh," Rice recalled. "He had a temperature of 103. The doctor had ordered him to bed for a three-day rest. That afternoon he got three hits and stole three bases, sliding into second and third on sore, battered flesh."

Cobb lacked Babe Ruth's power and Tris Speaker's grace, but many consider him the greatest ballplayer who ever lived. When Baseball's Hall of Fame was completed in Cooperstown, New York, in 1939, the first memento formally hung in the museum was a pair of baseball shoes with flashing spikes. "That takes care of Ty Cobb," the judges seemed to say. "Now let's see who else belongs in the Hall."

Cobb could beat an opponent a hundred ways. He played twenty-four years in the major leagues and had the highest lifetime batting average—.367. Twelve times he won the American League batting championship and three times he hit over .400. He averaged 37 stolen bases a season and stole 96 in 1915. More than once he reached first base and then stole his way around the diamond without the batter's swinging at a pitch. He loved to shout to a pitcher that he was going to steal on the next pitch—and then keep his promise.

Some old-timers have insisted that Cobb was even better as an outfielder. He usually played center, but one day he shifted to right and threw out three runners at first base. Another time he made a back dive into the bleachers after a fly ball, caught his spikes in the rope around the rail, landed on his neck, and still held the ball.

Cobb was highly superstitious, yet nothing could send him into a rage faster than to be called lucky. "I make my own luck!" he would shout. He was thinking of ways to beat his opponents every second he was on the field. He wore weighted shoes in spring training to help increase his speed, and he was the first man to swing extra bats before stepping to the plate.

No one hated to lose more than Cobb and he did everything in his power to avoid it. He had few, if any, close friends in base-ball. His only friends on the field were his bat and his spikes. Many pitchers threw beanballs at Cobb, but they usually threw just one apiece. Cobb would bunt down the first-base line and as the pitcher came over to field the ball, Cobb would try to run him down. "When he was in his prime," said Detroit manager Hugh Jennings, "he had half the American League scared stiff."

Ty Cobb was born on December 18, 1886, on a country estate in Narrow Banks County, Georgia. His father, W. H. Cobb, was a wealthy man and a state senator. He was as strong-willed as Ty and he insisted

Cobb's fine eyesight and amazing reflexes helped him achieve the highest lifetime batting average in history.

that the boy study law. The conflict between Ty and his father began when Ty maintained that he wanted to become a doctor.

Ty finally resolved the conflict by leaving home when he was seventeen to play base-ball. His hometown minister had developed his interest in the sport. Cobb spent less than two years in the minors. He joined the Tigers late in 1905 and immediately began building his reputation. "Get out of my way, you old goats!" Cobb would shout at his teammates during batting practice. "I'm a better ballplayer now than you'll ever be!"

By 1907 Cobb's boasts couldn't be disputed. He hit .350 that season and from then until he quit in 1928, his average never fell below .323. Cobb always felt that his two best years were 1911 and 1912, in which he hit .420 and .410, respectively. The 1912 season was memorable in another respect: Cobb caused the only mass player strike in baseball history. It began when he stormed into the stands and attacked a heckler who had been riding him mercilessly. Cobb was suspended indefinitely by the league president and the Tiger players promptly refused to play without him. Tiger officials put together a pick-up team, which lost to the A's, 24–2.

But Cobb's troubles weren't over. Later that season he was attacked by a trio of thugs, apparently in revenge for the beating he had given the heckler. Cobb was badly cut by a knife, but still fought off the men.

In 1918 he joined the army and worked his way up to the rank of captain in the Chemical Warfare Division, but World War I was over before he saw action. He returned to baseball in 1919 and hit .384 to win another league batting title.

Cobb became a playing manager in 1921 and quickly got results. He didn't have enough material to win a pennant, but he molded the Tigers into the best hitting team in the league though they had been next-to-last the previous season. He achieved his success by pitting player against player, forcing them into greatness through anger. It had always worked for Cobb himself and sometimes it worked for his players.

After the 1926 season Ty resigned as Tiger manager, but he still couldn't force himself to hang up his spikes. He played for two years with the A's, finally retiring after the 1928 season. But those who knew him best sensed that Cobb would have given anything to have discovered a magic

A determined young man, Cobb comes to bat in an early Tiger game dressed in the uniform of the day.

fountain of youth so that he could continue playing.

During the last few years of his life, Cobb was stricken with cancer. Doctors marveled at how he ignored pain that would have wracked lesser men. The few people close to Cobb began to notice a mellowing of the old man, but his crusty core remained till the end. Less than a year before he died someone asked him what he thought he could hit against modern pitchers.

"Oh," said Cobb, "I guess around .300."

"Is that all?" said the amazed questioner.

"Well," said Cobb, "you have got to remember that I'm seventy-three."

Bob Cousy

The three eighth-graders had discovered a new sport. They had just played basketball for the first time and they loved it. Now they wanted to play every day. But there was one problem. In their neighborhood in Queens, a part of New York City, it was difficult for boys as small as they were to get into a game. Basketball was generally played on city-park playgrounds and schoolyards, and the big high-school boys dominated the courts.

The three eighth-graders would go to the schoolyard and watch the older players. When the bigger boys rested for a minute or two, the eighth-graders would run onto the court and take a few shots. But they soon decided they had to play more than that. If only they could get a basketball, they could practice almost as often as they wanted.

They finally settled on a plan. One day the three boys—Bob Cousy, Wes Field and Angus Kennedy—came to the schoolyard with a fourth friend, Don Darnell. As usual, they watched while the high-school boys played. Finally, the bigger boys stopped to rest. Angus walked onto the court where the others had left the ball. Wes had already run over to the fence at the edge of the court; Bob was on the sidewalk on the other side of the fence, and Don was halfway down the block.

Angus picked up the ball and got set to shoot. Suddenly he whirled and threw the ball to Wes. Wes threw the ball over the fence to Bob, and Bob fired it down the block to Don. Before the big fellows knew what had happened, Angus, Wes and Bob had disappeared, and Don was sitting at home, holding a basketball.

Cousy steals the ball from the Lakers' Elgin Baylor.

The boys had their basketball at last—but not for long. Three days later, threatened with a beating by the high-school players, they returned the ball. But the big fellows agreed to let them borrow it.

Now Bob Cousy and his friends played basketball every day. Bob played the most. He was so serious about the game that he would shovel snow off the court to play in the winter. He would play, soaking wet, in a pouring rain; he would even play at night by the dim light of a street lamp.

"Basketball! Basketball! Basketball!" his mother said. "Can't you think of anything else? You'll kill yourself with this game."

But Bob Cousy could think of nothing else. He had been born in New York City

33

on August 9, 1928. Growing up there, he had played stickball and handball in the streets. In 1939 his family moved to Queens, outside the main part of the city. There he learned to play baseball. Then he discovered basketball.

When Bob entered Andrew Jackson High School in 1942, he tried out for the basketball team. But the coach said he was too small, and he failed to make the squad. He played anyway, receiving excellent instruction from a playground director, Morty Arkin. Eventually he made the team and soon was the star. As a senior he was picked as captain of the New York City all-star team.

Then his troubles began all over again. Though he was a star, he was only six feet tall. The prominent basketball colleges offered scholarships only to taller boys. Because he could not afford to go to college without a scholarship, he began to think he might never get to college at all.

Finally Holy Cross College in Worcester, Massachusetts, offered him a scholarship. He made the first team as a sophomore and as a junior he began to gain the attention of the basketball world. In an important game against Loyola of Chicago in his junior year, Cousy unveiled a new maneuver. With the score 57–57 and ten seconds left in the game, Bob drove downcourt with the ball. The man guarding him stayed with him step for step, his arms out and his body between Bob and the basket. The Loyola player was in position to block any shot Bob could make. Suddenly Cousy slapped the ball behind his back with his right hand and picked up the dribble with his left hand. The defender was caught off-guard. Bob broke free and swept in a left-handed hook shot to win the game. "I had never even thought of such a maneuver," Bob said afterward. "It just came the

moment the situation forced me into it. It was one of those cases when necessity is the mother of invention. I was amazed myself at what I had done."

The behind-the-back dribble became part of Bob's game and in time it became the most imitated maneuver in basketball. Bob used it through the rest of his All-America college career, and he used it when he became a pro with the Boston Celtics.

After leading Holy Cross to the NCAA championship, Bob joined the Celtics in 1950. "I hope you can make this team," Celtic coach Red Auerbach told him. "But if you can't, don't blame me. A little guy always has two strikes on him in this business. It's a big man's game."

Bob made the team and, as a pro, he really hit his peak. He did things with an original flair. He dribbled behind his back. He whipped passes behind his back. He did acrobatics that usually ended with his slipping the ball into the basket or with a teammate shooting an easy layup.

While playing with the Celtics, Cousy had hundreds of great moments. Perhaps his greatest came in 1953 when he scored 50 points against the Syracuse Nationals in a play-off game. Many players have scored more, but 25 of Cousy's 50 points came in overtime periods. He sank a foul shot to send the game into the first overtime, another foul shot to send it into the second, a one-hand shot from the keyhole to send it into the third and a midcourt hook shot to send it into the fourth. Then he scored nine of his team's twelve points in the fourth overtime, and Boston finally won the game.

From 1950, when Cousy joined the Celtics, until 1963, when he retired, the team won seven division championships and six league championships. He won the league's most valuable player trophy in 1957. He was on the All-NBA first team ten times and on the second team twice. He was basketball's greatest play-maker and also one of its greatest scorers. He scored 16,955 points and made an amazing total of 6,945 assists.

Cousy was a relentless competitor. Before a game he would sit alone in the locker room, rarely hearing anything, rarely speaking. Then in a semi-trance, he would go out and play full fury. After a game it took a full half-hour for him to regain his composure. Other times he was a thoroughly sociable man. He was friendly with fans, teammates and opponents and loved to play a practical joke or tell a good story.

Cousy was admired by NBA players for his high principles. When Chuck Cooper, one of the first Negroes in the NBA, was not allowed to stay in a southern hotel with the other Celtics, Cousy left the hotel and rode back to Boston with Cooper on an all-night train. When the NBA players decided they needed a pension plan, Cousy, although he needed no pension, led the fight and got them one.

After Cousy retired from the Celtics, he became the basketball coach at Boston College. In 1969 he moved back into the pros—as coach of the Cincinnati Royals. Bob, at age 41, even became an active player again, briefly, during his first season with the Royals. He wanted to show his players how to do it.

He remains the yardstick by which basketball people measure other stars. Even with Cousy in retirement, coaches still say, "Know how good that kid of mine is? He's as good as Cousy."

And, inevitably, people remember the day Red Auerbach heard such a statement, then rose in anger and bellowed, "I'm getting tired of this baloney. I've got news for you. There ain't nobody as good as Cooz. There never was."

High in the air, Cousy finds his target across court and cocks his arm to throw.

Celtics coach Red Auerbach doubted that Cousy would make it in the NBA, but Bob soon became his favorite player.

Glenn Cunningham

It was almost time for the big race. The cinder track was in near-perfect condition. A hint of a breeze ruffled the flags along the rim of Princeton University's Palmer Stadium. Everything on that late afternoon in June, 1934, seemed ideal. But as blue-jerseyed Glenn Cunningham jogged down the track in his warmup for the mile run, his left ankle gave way and he almost fell.

The crowd of 25,000 watched tensely, then murmured in disappointment. The wavy-haired graduate of Kansas University rubbed the swollen ankle briskly, scowled and limped painfully toward his dressing room under the huge concrete stands.

When the starter's pistol barked, however, Cunningham was ready at the starting line with the rest of the contestants. And by the time that gun went off again, signaling the start of the last lap, the sturdy little Kansan's murderous pace had wilted the competition. Spectators had expected to see Cunningham pound around the final turn in his familiar stretch kick, in pursuit of the long-legged pace-setter, Bill Bonthron. Instead they saw Cunningham forty yards ahead and still sprinting gamely for the tape. That wobbly ankle carried him across the finish line in 4 minutes, 6.7 seconds—a world record. "AMAZING TIME,"

Cunningham crosses the finish line in the AAU track and field meet in Princeton, New Jersey.

a New York newspaper headline stated the next morning.

"That ankle was swelled up like a popcorn ball," conceded Bill Hargiss, Cunningham's coach. But Hargiss was not amazed at Cunningham's record-breaking performance. He knew the full story of Glenn Cunningham's grit and determination.

Later, Cunningham suffered one of his worst defeats on that same Princeton track. In 1935 he lost in the mile to the sandy-haired New Zealander, Jack Lovelock. And in 1936, Lovelock scored another victory which Cunningham ached to win, in the Olympic 1500-meter run at Berlin. Lovelock, Cunningham and the next four finishers all clipped the previous record, but Cunningham lost the gold medal he wanted so badly. Because World War II wiped out plans for the 1940 Games, the Berlin 1500-meter run proved to be Cunningham's last chance at the medal.

The plucky Kansan later spoke of it as his toughest defeat. But he added promptly: "It wasn't the toughest moment of my life."

The awful moment that marked Glenn Cunningham from boyhood through manhood was the result of a terrible accident. Glenn had been born on August 4, 1909, on a farm in Kansas. When he started school, he trotted three miles over country roads to and from the schoolhouse in little Elkhart.

Each morning Glenn and his older brother, Floyd, built a fire in the school stove. One day when Glenn was only seven, flames suddenly billowed out of the stove and set the small schoolhouse on fire. The boys used kerosene to start the fire each morning, but someone had mistakenly filled the kerosene container with gasoline. Floyd died in the flames, and Glenn was burned so badly that doctors told him he might never walk again.

Glenn congratulates winner Jack Lovelock after the 1500-meter run at the 1936 Olympics.

After many weeks in bed, young Glenn dragged himself outside on crutches—legs scarred, pale skin stretched thinly over twisted ankles. When he put down the crutches, he later recalled, "My legs buckled under me. There was no strength in them. It was the most awful moment I've ever known." His embarrassed friends looked on sympathetically as Glenn blurted out: "I could run before, and I can still run. You guys just wait and see."

The road was long and painful, but Cunningham's vow came true. "I rubbed my legs every night and every morning," he said. "It hurt like thunder to walk, but it didn't hurt at all when I ran. So for five or six years, just about all I did was run."

When he was fourteen, he got a job loading wheat and began to build up his arms and chest as well as his legs. He had to train in tennis shoes, but he trained extra long. He ate steak and vegetables. He slept ten hours a night. And by the time he ran his last high-school mile,

Cunningham

Cunningham had sped to a United States interscholastic record of 4:24.7.

With his precise timing and powerful finishing surge, Cunningham soon dominated indoor track in this country. Some fans found his machinelike success unexciting, and even booed his appearances at New York's Madison Square Garden, where he won twenty-two indoor miles. His success on indoor tracks is especially amazing since the hard running surface and sharp turns put an extra strain on a runner's leg muscles.

Spectators thought he was showing off when he jogged incessantly up and down the track before a race, throwing back his head and snorting. But he wasn't even aware of the crowd. Because of the scar tissue and stretched muscles in his legs, Cunningham needed forty-five minutes to get ready for a race. He also admitted that he had a hard time getting used to smoke-filled arenas. He said the smoke bothered his breathing.

Cunningham's marvelous indoor record —six victories in the Wanamaker Mile, six in the Baxter Mile, five in the Columbian Mile—shows that the smoke could not have bothered him too much. But one night in 1938, when he asked an indoor crowd not to smoke, he cut loose with the fastest mile of his career.

Dartmouth College had asked Cunningham to try for a new mile record on its springy, high-banked indoor track. The large crowd respected his request not to smoke and the 28-year-old miler zeroed in on a new mark with the help of six Dartmouth runners who each ran part of the race with him and helped to set a fast pace. The result: a record-shattering mile in 4:04.4, four seconds lower than Cunningham's own indoor mark. "I've never received such support from a crowd in all my years of racing," he said afterward.

At the end of his running career in 1940, Cunningham became a teacher, lecturer and part-time lay preacher. Although he had ten children of his own, he and his wife opened a farm near Wichita for underprivileged youngsters, and before long found themselves using up their life savings. "On my speaking tours, I'd hear of a youngster who was having trouble or was close to becoming a delinquent," he said. "We'd have him sent out to the farm and take care of him as long as he wanted to stay."

In time, Cunningham's many records fell. He predicted that runners would someday conquer the four-minute mile. But these new achievements supported, in their own way, Glenn Cunningham's philosophy.

"The human race isn't getting any faster," he says. "It's just beginning to realize its potentialities."

Cunningham crosses the finish line 10 yards ahead in the 1937 Wanamaker Mile.

Dizzy Dean

Frank Frisch, the fiery manager and second baseman, was all business as he rose to his feet in the clubhouse. His St. Louis Cardinals, preparing to take the field for a doubleheader with Brooklyn, badly needed two victories, for they were fighting for the National League pennant and it was September 21st already. Frisch fixed his eyes on Dizzy Dean, who was to pitch the first game, and began to review the Brooklyn line-up.

"Keep the ball high and outside for Leslie," said Frisch. "He'll hit it over the fence if you get it inside."

"That ain't how I pitch to him," Dean piped up. Dean was twenty-three years old, a strapping man with a southern drawl and enough confidence for ten men. "I give him nothin' but low-and-inside stuff, and he ain't got a hit off me yet."

Frisch scowled and proceeded to the next Brooklyn name, Tony Cuccinello. "Nothing but curves for Tony. Tony'll slap a fast ball into the left-field lumber every time you give him one."

"That's mighty funny," mused Dean. "I never have bothered to dish him up a curve yet, and he's still tryin' for his first loud foul off Old Diz."

Frisch continued through the Brooklyn line-up, his face growing redder each time Dean contradicted him. Finally Dean said, "This is a silly business, Frank. I've won twenty-six games already this season and it don't look exactly right for an infielder like you to be tellin' a star like me how I should pitch."

Looking like a bird in flight, Dean begins his wind-up.

Frisch exploded. He told Dean to go ahead and pitch as he pleased but that he would be pounded off the mound. But Dean pitched so well that he didn't give up a hit until two men were out in the eighth inning. He gave up only three hits in the whole game.

The year was 1934, and Dizzy Dean was the talk of the land. Baseball fans did not know exactly where he had come from. He told one newspaperman he'd been born in Lucas, Arkansas, and told another that his birthplace was Holdenville, Oklahoma. To a third, he said Bond, Mississippi. "I wasn't going to have their bosses bawl 'em out for gettin' the same story," explained Diz. His parents had named him Jay Hanna Dean. But when one of his boyhood friends

died, he took the boy's name—Jerome Herman—as an act of affection. With his father, Diz spent his youth roaming the south, picking cotton for fifty cents a day.

Right-handed, Dizzy Dean was a blur of arms and legs on the mound. He reared 'way back, kicked his left foot high and fired the ball with blazing speed. In 1932, his first full season as a big leaguer, he won 18 games for the Cardinals, and in his first five years, he averaged 24 victories a year. To anyone who would listen, Diz announced that he could outpitch anyone in baseball. Many called him a blowhard but he replied, "It ain't braggin' if you can do it."

In the '34 season, Diz certainly managed to do it. That year, the Cardinals brought up his 20-year-old brother, Paul, also a pitcher. "Me and Paul," trumpeted Diz, "can win a pennant for St. Louis." Paul was as quiet as Diz was loud, but both men reduced enemy bats to absolute silence. The day Diz contradicted Frank Frisch's instructions and pitched a three-hitter, Paul pitched the second game of the double-header and achieved a no-hitter. "If you'd-a-told me you was going to pitch a no-hitter," Diz chided him, "why, I'd-a-pitched one, too." Paul had won 19 games and Diz had won 30 when the Cardinals entered the World Series against the Detroit Tigers.

Diz pleaded for permission to start every game, insisting he could wrap up the Series early if given a chance. When told it was impossible for him to pitch every day and win four straight games, he replied, "Maybe

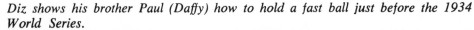

Diz shows his brother Paul (Daffy) how to hold a fast ball just before the 1934 World Series.

so, but I'll win four out of five." Before taking the field for the opening game, Diz blithely got into the pre-game festivities by taking a place in the band and puffing away on a tuba.

Then, ambling past the Detroit dugout, Diz spotted slugger Hank Greenberg and said: "What makes you so white? Boy, you're a-shakin' like a leaf. I get it. You heard that Old Diz was goin' to pitch. Well, you're right. It'll be all over in a few minutes. Old Diz is goin' to pitch, and he's goin' to pin your ears back."

Greenberg blasted a home run off Old Diz, but Diz himself smashed a double and beat the Tigers on an eight-hitter, 8-3.

Of course Frisch refused to let Diz pitch every game, so the next day Diz sat on the bench and watched the Tigers even the Series. Paul pitched the Cardinals to victory in the third game, and in the fourth Detroit again squared the Series. Diz did not pitch that day but Frisch put him into the game as a pinch runner. While on base, he was cut down by an infield throw that struck him squarely on the forehead. He was rushed to a hospital to have his head X-rayed. One newspaper reported the next day that the X-rays "showed nothing."

Diz pitched a six-hitter in the fifth game but lost, 3-1. Then Paul turned in a seven-hit victory to deadlock the Series at three games apiece. Now it was up to Diz in the final game. Before the game, Diz informed the Tiger manager that there was no chance of beating him.

Diz proved as tough as his word but as nonchalant as ever. With Greenberg at bat, Frisch barked at Diz, "Don't give him anything chest high!"

Diz promptly sailed the ball chest high, and Greenberg cracked a frightening line drive to center field. "Hey, Frank, you was right," Diz called out cheerfully. But when the game was over he had shut out the Tigers on six hits, 11-0, to win the Series.

In the next two years Dizzy Dean won 28 and 24 games, but in the 1937 All-Star game he broke his toe. Changing his pitching motion to compensate for the injury, he ruined his arm. St. Louis traded him to the Chicago Cubs the next year, and though he could not throw hard, he helped the Cubs win the pennant.

Talkative as ever, Dizzy Dean's ultimate destiny was broadcasting. First in radio and then in TV, he brought his Ozarks style to baseball announcing: "The runner just slud into third base safely . . . This is what you call a real slugger's fest."

School teachers protested that his use of the word "ain't" exerted an undesirable influence on children. Diz answered, in all sincerity, that he hoped no one would fall into the ungrammatical ways of a man who had not gone past second grade. But then, unable to remain serious for long, he quickly quoted his favorite American humorist, Will Rogers:

"A lot of people who don't say ain't, ain't eatin'."

Just off second base, Dean drops in his tracks after being beaned by an infield throw during the 1934 Series.

Jack Dempsey

It was September, 1927. In Chicago's Soldiers Field, 104,000 people had been lucky enough to get seats for the big heavyweight boxing match. Across the continent, fifty million others strained close to their radios, trying to hear the announcer's voice over the shouting and the static. The Dempsey-Tunney fight was one of the first ever to be broadcast to a large audience.

From 1919 to 1926, Jack Dempsey had been heavyweight champion of the world, knocking out opponents fifty pounds heavier with his pounding fists. Then in 1926, Gene Tunney, a quick and clever boxer, had outjabbed Dempsey for ten rounds and

taken the title away from him. Now, a year later, Dempsey was determined to win back that title.

For six rounds Tunney jabbed and ran away, piling up points. But in the seventh, Dempsey came rushing in at him, swinging a left hook that ripped across the champion's mouth. Tunney spun against the ropes, and Dempsey hit him with his right. The champion's eyes went glassy and he crashed to the canvas. The crowd roared. Dempsey hovered over the fallen champion, fists cocked to batter him again if he should rise before the count of 10.

But the referee wasn't counting! He was motioning to Dempsey to go to a neutral corner. Dempsey had forgotten a rule which required that a fighter scoring a knockdown go to a neutral corner before

The famous long count—the stunned Gene Tunney has time to recover as the referee points Dempsey to the neutral corner.

the count could start. Dempsey rushed to a corner, but five seconds had already ticked away. The referee finally started to count and, at 9, Tunney rose, groggy. He had been on the floor for at least fourteen seconds.

Dempsey rushed at him, but Tunney hung on through the seventh and through the last three rounds, winning the decision. Afterward he claimed he would have risen at the count of 9 even if Dempsey had gone to the corner and the count had started immediately. But Dempsey fans argue to this day that the "long count" gave Tunney time to recover.

Dempsey should not have stood over Tunney. But that was his nature. He knew no other way to fight. When he knocked a man down, he would stand waiting to get him again when he got up. "What do you want me to do?" he once asked a critic. "Write him a letter that I'm going to hit him?"

Dempsey had been fighting that way since boyhood. He was born on June 24, 1895, in Manassa, Colorado, a gold-mining town. The ninth of eleven children, he was named William by his parents. For years the Dempsey family drifted by wagon all over the west, Jack's father taking whatever odd jobs he could find.

Jack had little formal schooling. His father taught him how to hunt, fish and set traps and how to track game through bush. Jack's brother, Barney, taught him how to fight, because if a boy in the tough mining towns couldn't fight, he'd be beaten up by every bully in town. Jack could soon outfight anyone. Sometimes, just for the exercise, he and another boy would go into the woods and slug at each other, bare-fisted, for hours.

At sixteen, he decided to run away from his family. He got jobs working the deep

veins in gold mines in Colorado, Utah and Nevada. Calling himself Jack Dempsey, the name of a former great fighter, he roamed the gold fields looking for fights. Although he weighed only 165 pounds, he took on 200-pound heavyweights and knocked out most of them.

Late in 1916 Jack came to New York. Before he had been in the city long, a wise old ring pro smashed two of his ribs. Dempsey hastily left town, working his way west by fighting and hopping freight trains when he had no money. In San Francisco he met Jack "Doc" Kearns, a skilled fight promoter. Kearns saw greatness in this six-foot hobo, who was now a muscular 190 pounds. He taught Dempsey the basics of boxing, then shrewdly matched him against inept fighters so that Dempsey could practice the basics before he met top competition.

Kearns began a publicity campaign, calling his "Manassa Mauler" the "toughest man ever to come out of the west." In 1918 and 1919 Jack Dempsey made the nation believe the claim by knocking out twenty-seven of the best heavyweights in the country. On July 4, 1919, he stepped into a ring in Toledo, Ohio, to face 6-foot, 6-inch, 250-pound Jess Willard, the heavyweight champion of the world. The 190-pound Dempsey lashed into the huge Willard like a crazy tiger, knocking him down seven times in the first round and breaking Willard's cheekbone in thirteen places. In the third round, the dazed Willard was hanging on the ropes. His seconds threw in the towel, and Jack Dempsey was the champion of the world.

For the next five years, Dempsey chopped up challenger after challenger. The peak of his career came on September 14, 1923, in front of 82,000 screaming fans at New York's old Polo Grounds. That night Dempsey battled 220-pound Luis Firpo of

Knocked through the ropes by Firpo, Dempsey lands upside down on ringside reporters.

A few seconds later in the same fight, Firpo goes down for nine.

Argentina, known as the Wild Bull of the Pampas.

Five seconds after the bell, Firpo knocked Dempsey down. He got up and knocked Firpo down. Firpo got up and staggered Dempsey. Dempsey knocked Firpo down a second, third, fourth, fifth and sixth time —and the first round was less than two minutes old.

Staggering, Firpo got to his feet, charged across the ring and smashed Dempsey through the ropes. He fell into the typewriters of reporters at ringside but the reporters hoisted him back into the ring before the count of 10. The bell rang. In the second round Dempsey flattened Firpo once, then again. It was the ninth knockdown in a little more than three minutes. But this time the gallant Firpo was counted out.

In that fight Dempsey had stood over Firpo and knocked him down each time he stood up. Horrified officials wrote a new rule ordering boxers to go to a neutral corner after each knockdown. It was this rule that may have led to Dempsey's defeat in the 1927 match when he tried to reclaim the title from Tunney.

After the Tunney fight, Dempsey announced his retirement, though he made brief "comeback tours" in 1931 and again in 1940. His record: 65 victories in 70 fights, including 48 knockouts. He earned well over three million dollars.

Later Dempsey bought a New York restaurant where he often serves famous sports celebrities. And many years after he lost the "long-count" fight to Tunney, he got a measure of revenge. In 1950 the Associated Press asked sports writers to name the greatest fighter of the half-century. The writers considered Tunney and Joe Louis and all the rest. But their choice— Jack Dempsey.

Joe DiMaggio

Pitcher Bobo Newsom decided one day to probe for Joe DiMaggio's weakness as a hitter. The first time up, Joe hit a home run. Then he finished the game with three consecutive doubles off Newsom.

"I finally discovered Joe DiMaggio's weakness," Bobo hollered in the locker room. "Two-base hits."

Newsom's "discovery" almost summed up the success other pitchers had had in getting DiMaggio out. Bob Feller of Cleveland was the greatest pitcher of DiMaggio's era, yet Feller's manager, Lou Boudreau, once said that he would rather use a lesser pitcher against DiMaggio. "When it comes down to Feller against DiMaggio," said Boudreau, "DiMaggio always gives it a little extra."

In thirteen seasons with the New York Yankees DiMaggio's average was .325. His batting stance—legs spread wide, bat grasped firmly just off the shoulder—was copied on every sandlot in America. Twice he led the American League in hitting, with averages of .381 and .352. And twice he led in home runs.

But hitting represented only a fraction of DiMaggio's skills. "There may have been guys who could hit as well," American League president Joe Cronin has said. "But nobody had Joe's all-round ability to hit, run, field, throw and produce in the clutch."

Casey Stengel, who managed the Yankees near the end of DiMaggio's career, liked to tell of the only time Joe was thrown out trying to take an extra base. "Joe tried to

Joe's easy grace at bat and in the field earned him the nickname "The Yankee Clipper."

45

slide into second under the tag," said Casey. "Art Passarella, the umpire, called him out and knew he had made a mistake. Joe was nice about it. He just asked Art to hold his decision on him in the future, to take a moment longer to make sure. Passarella must have passed the word around to the other boys in blue because DiMaggio never was called out in that situation again."

They called DiMaggio "The Yankee Clipper," after the stately sailing ships of the 1800s. No sailing vessel ever moved with more effortless grace than DiMaggio in the field. "Joe did everything so naturally," Stengel has said, "that half the time he gave the impression he wasn't trying. He had the greatest instinct of any ballplayer I ever saw. He made the rest of them look like plumbers."

Stengel could talk about DiMaggio for hours, telling how Joe never threw to a wrong base and how he would make a sensational catch to pull a pitcher out of a hole. Connie Mack, baseball's Grand Old Man, summed up the general feeling about Joe when he said, "DiMaggio is the greatest team player of all time." Supporting Mack's praise are DiMaggio's three Most Valuable Player awards.

Strangely, Joe always insisted that one of his brothers may have had more natural baseball ability than he did. He wasn't referring to Vince or Dom, who both played in the major leagues. He was talking about his oldest brother, Tom, who went to work on a fishing boat at an early age and never played professional baseball.

Fishing and baseball are inseparable in the DiMaggio family history. Joe's father was a fisherman on a small island off the coast of southern Italy before moving the family to San Francisco. But Joe, who was born on November 25, 1914, had no stomach for the sea. The smell of fish nauseated

him, something his father couldn't understand.

Joe, however, didn't have to worry about spending his life on a fishing boat. When he was eighteen, he signed with the San Francisco Seals of the Pacific Coast League. Ironically, the Seals had to sell Vince DiMaggio to Hollywood to make room for Joe. An immediate success, Joe hit safely in sixty-one consecutive games to establish a Pacific Coast League record.

Then one day Joe's world collapsed. Hurrying out of a taxi, he suddenly fell to the pavement. He severely sprained some tendons. "I went down as though I were shot," he recalls. "There were four sharp cracks. The pain was terrific."

Joe played the next day against doctors' orders—and hit a home run. But he was through for the season. His value on the major league market plummeted and only the Yankees were still interested in him. Through the urging of Bill Essick, a Yankee scout, New York bought DiMaggio for $25,000 and five players.

It was a steal. Joe joined the Yankees in 1936 and had one of the most impressive rookie seasons ever. After missing the first seventeen games because he had burned himself under a diathermy machine, he went on to hit .323 and drive in 125 runs. New York won the pennant and the World Series. The DiMaggio era had begun.

In just one season Joe proved he was the finest center fielder in baseball. In the years that followed he established a permanent place in baseball. There was, for example, the catch he made on August 2, 1939, against Detroit. DiMaggio always considered it his best one.

Hank Greenberg hit a high fly ball which looked as though it might drop into the center-field bleachers. DiMaggio tore after it, his back to the infield. Somehow he managed to get behind the Yankee Stadium flagpole. When he got within two feet of the bleacher wall, he stuck up his glove. The ball dropped in and Joe squeezed it, just a step before he hit the wall. Joe heard the crowd roaring and he looked at the ball in his glove. No one could believe he had caught it, and neither could he.

In 1941 Joe set a record many experts feel may be the most durable of all baseball records. DiMaggio hit safely in 56 straight games. It was an incredible feat when you consider all the elements that could have stopped the streak: fancy fielding plays, bases on balls, long hits which go foul by inches, well-hit balls which go directly at a fielder. In the fortieth game Joe had to contend with a pitcher—Johnny Babich of the Athletics—who seemed determined not

to give Joe anything to hit. After Babich got him out in the first inning, the pitcher started throwing curve balls two and three feet away from the plate. With the count 3–0, the pitch was inside and high. Joe swung anyway and it went through the box to center field for a double. "When I was standing on second base," Joe said later, "I happened to look at Babich. He was as white as a ghost. The ball hadn't missed him by much."

Joe's streak finally ended on July 17th when the Cleveland third baseman, Ken Keltner, made fine stops of two hard-hit balls down the foul line. DiMaggio hit safely in the next sixteen games and someone pointed out to Joe that if Keltner hadn't robbed him, he would have had a 73-game record. "You can't figure it that way," said

Despite injuries, Joe continued to lead the Yankees. Here he crosses the plate after hitting a home run in 1947.

An alert base runner, Joe executes a hook slide into second base. He was safe for a double.

Joe with characteristic modesty. "I could have been stopped almost anywhere along the line."

In 1942 he played on another pennant winner, but this time the Yankees lost the World Series to the St. Louis Cardinals. It was the only losing World Series Joe would experience in ten tries and he took it exceptionally hard. "I don't think I ever felt so low in my life," he said. "After all, we were the Yankees—we weren't supposed to be beaten."

It was typical of DiMaggio that he would mourn for a losing team effort and try to brush off any personal disappointments. He never made excuses for himself, even when there was plenty of opportunity. When he returned to the Yankees in 1946, after three years in the Army, he was not at his physical best. Bone spurs in the heel of his foot began to hobble him, and the pain at times was excruciating. But he bore the agony in stoic silence. In 1949 an operation cut his season in half, yet he still hit .346 in the 76 games he played.

It was clear that DiMaggio now was playing on borrowed time. He was no longer a full-time player and before the 1951 season, he hinted to some writers that this would probably be his last year. When he hit .263—only his second time below .300—he chose to retire. He left an impressive legacy in the record books, including the fact that he was never thrown out of a ball game for protesting an official decision.

Even the umpires got sentimental when Joe DiMaggio retired.

Bob Feller

Bob Feller, seventeen years old and a high-school junior, stood out on the mound, staring down at the St. Louis Cardinal batter, Leo Durocher. "Keep the ball in the park, busher," snarled Durocher. Feller nervously tightened his grip on the ball.

This was no dream. This was actually happening. Feller was on a big league mound, pitching to the famous St. Louis Cardinal Gashouse Gang: Dizzy Dean, Frankie Frisch, Leo Durocher, Pepper Martin.

It had all happened just as Bob's father had said it would. Back home in Van Meter, Iowa, people had laughed when Bob's father had talked about his son's pitching in the big leagues. But he had seen something special in the way Bob threw a ball, even as a child of three.

Bob had been born on November 3, 1918, in his father's farmhouse near Van Meter. Soon Bob was insisting that his mother buy him a rubber ball whenever she took him into town. When he returned to the farm, he would throw the ball against the side of a barn for hours.

When Bob was ten, his father bought him a baseball uniform, spikes, bats, baseballs, a catcher's mitt and a fielder's glove. Bob became the manager of the Van Meter baseball team, mainly because he owned the bulk of the equipment they used. He was also the shortstop and cleanup hitter. "In those days," he says, "I thought I was a great slugger."

It was Bob's father who first suggested that his son try pitching. Bob wasn't very interested. As a pitcher he wouldn't be able to play in every game But his father convinced him that a pitcher is tremendously

Bob was pitching for the Indians before his eighteenth birthday.

important even if he plays less often. In the spring of 1932 Bob and his father laid out a baseball diamond on the farm and organized a team, the Oakviews, with 13-year-old Bob as pitcher. His fast ball soon became a whizzing, frightening thing to batters. Three years later he was a strapping 5 feet, 11 inches tall and weighed 175 pounds, and he was striking out 20 batters a game for a Des Moines semiprofessional team.

One hot July day in 1935, Bob was driving a tractor over his father's fields when he saw a slim man pushing his way through the corn. The man was Cy Slapnicka, a scout for the Cleveland Indians. The next day Slapnicka watched Bob strike out a dozen batters. He and Bob's father came to an agreement: the next summer

Bob would pitch for an Indian minor league team.

But in the spring of 1936 Bob had a sore arm. "Keep him home and don't let him pitch," Slapnicka wrote to Bob's father. In June Bob went to Cleveland. A trainer massaged the soreness out of his arm, and Cleveland officials decided to keep Bob for a trial.

The trial came in July, during an exhibition game against the Cardinals. Bob came into the game in the fourth inning and struck out Durocher and six other Cardinals in three innings. The Bob Feller strikeout story had begun.

In Washington several weeks later, he was told to warm up in the bullpen. "After throwing awhile," said Bob years later, "my arm was warm but my blood was cold." Still he went into the game and gave up no hits over two innings. On August 23,

1936, he started his first big league game. He struck out fifteen batters and won the game, 4–1. A few weeks later he struck out seventeen men, tying the big league record.

When the 1936 season ended, Bob went back to Van Meter High School for his senior year. The next spring, with a tutor helping him with his school work, he began setting a string of pitching records. Wild and blazing fast—his fast ball once was timed at 100 miles an hour—he had batters edging nervously away from the plate. When they began looking for the fast ball, he would throw a dipping curve ball that looked, according to hitters, as if "it fell off a table." Wild pitches and bases on balls cost him some games in the 1937 season, but he finished with a 9 and 7 record.

He was still wild in 1938. In one game

A batter's eye view of a Feller pitch. His fast ball was once clocked at 95 miles per hour.

he struck out a record number of 18 batters, but lost the game. During the season he won 17 games, lost 11. But by 1939 he had mastered pinpoint control. He won 24 games and lost only 9. On opening day of 1940 he threw a no-hitter against the White Sox, going on to win 27 games that year. In 1941, he won 25 games.

On December 7, 1941, the Japanese struck at Pearl Harbor, and the next day the United States entered World War II. On December 9, Bob Feller enlisted in the Navy. As a chief in gunnery on the battleship *Alabama,* he fought Nazi submarines in the Atlantic and Japanese fighters in the Pacific.

Late in 1945 he came out of the service. His playing looked rusty and, at the start of the 1946 season, newspapers flashed this headline over a wire-service story: FELLER FAST BALL IS GONE. Just a week later Feller came into New York to face the mighty Yankees. He hurled the fast ball past the Yankees in inning after inning and, when it was all over, Feller had a 1–0 victory and his second no-hitter. "I guess you still have the fast ball, Bob," said the sheepish reporter who had written the story. In 1946, Feller struck out 348 batters, setting a record that has been topped since only by Sandy Koufax.

In 1948 he won 19 games and Cleveland captured its first American League pennant in 28 years. The Indians also took the World Series, defeating the Boston Braves, but Feller was beaten twice. The first time he lost by a heartbreaking 1–0.

In 1951 he pitched his third no-hitter, a record that stood until Sandy Koufax pitched his fourth no-hitter in 1965. In 1954 Feller won ten games to help Cleveland win another pennant. But the one prize that had eluded him—a World Series triumph—would never be his. The Giants

Even the best men sometimes lose. Here Feller walks off the mound in a 1955 game. Manager Al Lopez waits for the new pitcher.

swept the 1954 Series in four games, and Feller never got a chance to start.

Still he had almost everything else: a record 11 one-hitters, 266 victories, six 20-win seasons and a place in the Hall of Fame. He retired in 1956.

Today he lives in a suburb of Cleveland with his wife, Virginia, and is the owner of a prosperous insurance firm. Although he was the greatest right-hander of his time, the glory has not changed Bob Feller much. There is still some of the country boy in the way he walks and talks.

From that first strikeout of Lippy Leo Durocher, Feller was a big league star, and the people in Van Meter, Iowa, quickly learned how right Bob's father had been.

Lou Gehrig

Lou Gehrig was born in Manhattan on June 19, 1903. Even as a youth he liked the noise and lights and action of the city where he was to live all his life.

When Lou entered high school, his parents were working at a Columbia University fraternity house—his mother as a cook; his father as a handyman. Before leaving for classes in the morning, Lou would go up to Columbia and help prepare breakfast for the fraternity boys. In the evening, he would come back to Columbia, wait on tables and clean the kitchen. But as much as he helped his parents, he wanted to help them more. One day he told them he was going to quit school so he could get a full-time job.

"No," his mother said. "You must have a college education."

So he worked, went to classes, studied and even played ball. He played on the Commerce High School football, soccer and basketball varsities. But as good as he was at these sports, baseball was his best game. He was a big, powerful boy, standing six-feet, one-inch tall and weighing 190 pounds. Even then he could hit the ball astounding distances, especially at crucial moments.

In June of 1920 Lou's baseball team won the New York City high-school championship and rode in a Pullman to Chicago to play that city's champion, Lane Tech. In the ninth inning, with the score 8–8 and the bases loaded, Lou walked to the plate. He settled into his left-handed stance, swung hard and hit the ball out of the park, winning the game. The park was Wrigley Field, home of the Chicago Cubs.

In the fall Lou became a student at Columbia University, where he was soon the star of the baseball team. One day he hit a ball out of the Columbia stadium, across 116th Street and onto the steps of Butler Library. The home run so impressed New York Yankee scout Paul Krichell that Krichell telephoned the Yankee executive offices and announced that he had discovered another Babe Ruth. Krichell eventually signed Lou to a Yankee contract and in the spring of 1923 Lou came to his first major league training camp.

The Yankees saw immediately that Lou had the potential to become a star. They decided that first base would be his best position, but they already had an excellent first baseman, Wally Pipp. Since Lou was, after all, only twenty years old, they sent him to the minor leagues for experience. He played in the minors most of the '23

After an amazing college career and two years in the minors, Lou joined the Yankees in 1925.

52

and '24 seasons, then joined the Yankees permanently in 1925.

On June 1, 1925, Lou got into a game as a pinch hitter. On June 2, Yankee manager Miller Huggins walked up to Lou in the locker room. "Pipp has a headache," he said. "You're playing first base today."

Lou played first base that day, and the next day, and the day after that. Soon the days stretched into seasons. Lou played while others rested. He played with broken fingers and pulled muscles, he played in important games and unimportant games. He walloped booming homers, drove in hundreds of runs and hit for high batting averages. Everyone agreed that Babe Ruth was the number one slugger in baseball, but the fans also agreed that the Babe's teammate, Lou Gehrig, was number two. Babe was up third in the Yankee batting order and Lou was up fourth and the two of them were the heart of the batting order known as "Murderers' Row."

In 1927 Lou batted .373 and in 1928 he batted .374. He had 47 home runs in 1927, 46 in 1931 and 49 in 1936. He led the American League with 175 runs batted in in 1927, 142 in 1928, 175 in 1930 and 184 in 1931. He batted .545 in the 1928 World Series. On June 3, 1932, he hit four home runs in a nine-inning game, tying a record that was still unbroken more than thirty years later.

As good as he was, though, he never got much publicity. First, he was overshadowed by Ruth; then, after Ruth retired, he was overshadowed by Joe DiMaggio. "I'm not a headline guy," he once said. He and his wife went to concerts rather than nightclubs and they preferred dining at home to dining in famous restaurants. They shunned the spotlight.

Lou came into the spotlight, however, in July, 1933. One day that month, baseball

Gehrig's booming bat earned him three Most Valuable Player awards.

writer Dan Daniel discovered that Gehrig had played in every Yankee game since June 1, 1925. "You've played in 1,252 consecutive games," Lou was told. "The record is 1,307." Nobody had realized that he was that close.

Lou broke the record. And he kept playing in game after game. Soon he had played in 1,500 consecutive games, then 2,000. Suddenly, in the 1938 season, though he was still in every game, he was playing

Four of the Yankees' famous Murderer's Row—(l. to r.) Gehrig, Carl Coombs, Tony Lazzeri and Babe Ruth.

poorly. He couldn't whip the bat around the way he once had, and he couldn't scoop up low throws or dig out grounders with his old agility. Nobody knew what was wrong.

Lou was the Yankee captain and was still adding games to his record streak, so manager Joe McCarthy did not want to take him out of the line-up. But Gehrig refused to get by on his reputation. On May 2, 1939, he took himself out of the line-up. His streak ended at 2,130 games, a record that no player has ever approached.

Doctors diagnosed Lou's trouble as amyotrophic lateral sclerosis, an incurable kind of paralysis. People couldn't believe

it when they heard that the indestructible Lou Gehrig, the man they called "The Iron Horse," was dying.

Courage had always been a part of Lou's life, and he was not about to lose it now. On July 4, 1939, the Yankees honored him with a "Gehrig Appreciation Day" at Yankee Stadium. Lou stood on the baseball field and spoke into a microphone. He would be dead in two years, but his words would not be forgotten.

"I may have been given a bad break," Lou said that day, "but I have an awful lot to live for. With all this, I consider myself the luckiest man on the face of this earth."

54

Pancho Gonzales

"I said to my son, you can take your choice. One of these three things you must do: Go back to school, take a job or get out of the house."

For Richard "Pancho" Gonzales there could be only one possible choice to this ultimatum laid down by his father, Manuel, in January, 1947. Pancho had just returned from the Navy. He had never liked school and had no skills that would help him get a job. So he left home. Knowing more about tennis than anything, he soon entered a tournament where he gained fame almost overnight. His decision to leave home set him on the way to becoming one of the four or five best players of all time.

His feats were especially noteworthy because Pancho was competing in a sport that is usually dominated by the wealthy. By contrast, Pancho's parents were poor people, who came to Los Angeles from Mexico in 1918. He was born in 1928 and six more Gonzales children followed. Although the family was never in want, there was no extra money for luxuries.

When he was twelve, Pancho's mother gave him a fifty-cent tennis racket for Christmas. He began hanging around tennis courts, where he struck up a friendship with a boy named Charles Pate. Charley

After serving, Pancho watches for the return with intense concentration.

had a newspaper route, and gave Pancho a better racket and some balls in return for help with the paper delivery.

Gonzales began to play in boys' tournaments when he was fourteen. A year later he caught the eye of Perry Jones, the ruler of Southern California tennis, who offered the lad coaching and tournament opportunities. But to play in Jones's tourneys, a boy had to be approved by his school principal as scholastically eligible. Pancho definitely was not. Most of the time he had not even been going to school. Jones advised Gonzales to go back to school and study if he wanted to play in the tournaments. Pancho tried, but he couldn't stay interested. He finally left school for good in the tenth grade. Tennis then occupied him until he entered the Navy in 1945.

When he returned home, Gonzales' father gave him the ultimatum of finding a job or leaving home. Pancho left home and turned to tennis. He entered a Southern California tournament using a friend's application since he had not been invited. Pancho got to the final round, where he took a set from Jack Kramer, a fellow Californian who was then the amateur tennis champion of the United States. Kramer, also a Navy veteran, had first won the amateur title in 1946. He was to win again in 1947 and then turn professional. Jack had the overpowering service and smashing forehand that had been the trademark of such great California players as Don Budge and Ellsworth Vines. Although Pancho finally lost the match to Kramer, he gained the attention of the tennis world.

His play in the Southern California event earned him an eastern tournament tour in the summer of 1947 with all expenses paid. He won no important matches, but played everywhere. When Pancho headed east again in the summer of 1948, he had a king-sized chip on his shoulder. As a poor man and a Mexican, he felt he was at a disadvantage among wealthy, society-conscious tennis followers. He felt that they singled him out for special abuse. Even his nickname was a burden. In California, "Pancho" was a derisive nickname for any Mexican.

Some sports writers made the situation worse. In the year since Pancho had gained national attention, all kinds of yarns had been told about him. Pancho insisted that most of them were not true, but it upset him to have to deny them again and again.

After only two seasons of play in top amateur tennis, Gonzales won the Nationals at Forest Hills, New York. It seemed incredible. He was just twenty, the second youngest player to win the Nationals title. He had risen from number seventeen to number one in only ten days.

In this tournament Gonzales suddenly got control of his always powerful game. His blistering service, once timed at 112 miles per hour, was the key to his success. In addition, the direction of Pancho's service was beautifully disguised. With these advantages Gonzales could usually control the net either with a volley or an overhead smash. Pancho was also great at counterattacking. Often he would return for a winner a ball that his foe thought he had put out of play. His wonderful reflexes repeatedly got him out of difficult situations.

Now with the national title in hand, Pancho went into an unbelievable nosedive, losing half a dozen matches in a row. He was called the "greatest cheese champion in American tennis history." But Gonzales returned to Forest Hills in September, 1949, and silenced his critics by again winning the title with a five-set victory over Ted Schroeder.

Even with his second straight United

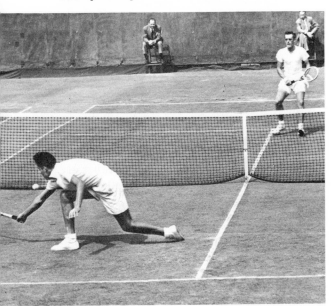

(Top) Gonzales follows through on the bullet-like serve that made him famous. (Bottom) Pancho (foreground) lunges to return Frank Parker's shot during the 1949 National Tennis Championships.

States championship, the kid from the other side of the tracks was still not fully accepted. In other years the winner was the guest of honor at a dinner held after the tournament. Not this time. Pancho and his wife, Henrietta, ate alone in the West Side Tennis Club. Only a few people even stopped at their table to offer congratulations.

Fifteen days later Pancho signed a $60,000 one-year contract to oppose the professional champion, Jack Kramer, on a nationwide tour. Jack trounced him, 94 matches to 29. Gonzales made excuses for his losses although he was never able to beat Kramer regularly. Later, when Kramer became tour promoter, he and Gonzales met in a court of law to wrangle over Pancho's contract.

But when Kramer retired from competition in 1954, Gonzales became the uncontested professional champion. For the next eight years he defeated the world's finest players: Frank Sedgman, Tony Trabert, Ken Rosewall, Lew Hoad and Pancho Segura.

Gonzales retired, several times in fact, to concentrate on teaching the sport he loved. But he repeatedly returned to active competition. In 1969, at the age of 41, Pancho won the longest match ever played at Wimbledon. It took him more than five hours to defeat 25-year-old Charles Pasarell, 22–24, 1–6, 16–14, 6–3, 11–9.

Gonzales continued to amaze fellow players and spectators with his powerful serve. And even into the 1970s, at an age when most athletes look toward their pensions, Pancho was still winning prize money on the pro circuit.

Pancho had come a long way from his days as a truant in Los Angeles. Not only had he become a great tennis player but he had proved that tennis was a game for the poor as well as the rich.

Red Grange

When Harold Grange was five years old, he had a dog named Jack. Harold would chase Jack all over the backyard, trying to trap the dog in a corner. Years later Harold "Red" Grange said: "Jack was unquestionably the greatest open-field runner I ever saw. I learned things from Jack I never forgot."

"Red" Grange, who got his nickname from the color of his hair, learned his lessons well. As a left halfback for the University of Illinois, he would soon dazzle the country with his open-field running, earning another nickname—the "Galloping Ghost." Bursting around end with jetlike speed, he would race from one sideline to the other, stopping and starting like a gust of wind. He left his tacklers sprawled on the ground behind him.

The six-foot, 170-pound ghost never galloped more artfully than on an October afternoon in 1924 against an unbeaten University of Michigan team. Before the game Michigan's coach, Fielding Yost, told reporters: "Mr. Grange will be carefully watched every time he takes the ball. There will be eleven clean, hard Michigan tacklers headed for him."

The Ghost took the opening kickoff at his 5-yard line and sped upfield along the right sideline. At the 20 he cut to the opposite sideline, weaving like a runaway snake; then he turned upfield, the entire Michigan team puffing behind him, and went all the way untouched for a 95-yard touchdown.

The Michigan banners sagged. They dropped to ground level minutes later when Grange went wide around end and galloped 67 yards for another touchdown. They disappeared altogether when Grange ran 56 yards for another touchdown and Illinois led, 20-0, after one period.

But Grange still wasn't through. He went 45 yards up the middle for his fourth touchdown. Then he threw a 12-yard touchdown pass. Finally, late in the game, he ran 40 yards to the Michigan 18-yard line from which he threw his second scoring pass. Illinois won, 39–14; the carefully watched Mr. Grange threw or ran for all six Illinois touchdowns.

Oddly, Grange went to Illinois doubting he would make the football team. He had always been a scrawny boy, but he came from hardy stock. His father, a burly six-footer, had been the boss of a lumber camp in Forksville, Pennsylvania, where Red was born on June 13, 1903. When Red was five years old, his mother died. He and his father moved from Forksville to Wheaton, Illinois, not far from Chicago. Years later his father would become the chief of the one-man Wheaton police department.

The kids in Wheaton played football on a field laid out on a hill. The 50-yard line was at the top and the goal lines were at the bottom on opposite sides of the hill. At kickoff, Red remembers, "You'd be standing at the bottom of the hill and the ball would come sailing out of nowhere from the other side. As you ran up the hill, the opposition would appear at the top and attack like the charge of the Light Brigade."

In 1922 Red enrolled at the University of Illinois, after a wild, running career as a high-school varsity man. At football practice that fall, weighing only 166 pounds, he looked around and said to himself: "What chance have I got against all these big guys?"

He was about to give up but his fraternity brothers insisted that he try to make the

58

team. To his surprise, he was still on the squad after it was cut from 160 to 50. And when the freshmen scrimmaged the varsity, Red scored on two long touchdown runs, beating a shocked varsity, 21–19, and giving the fans at Illinois a preview of what was to come.

As a sophomore in 1923, wearing the number 77 that he would make famous, Red was a starter in the opening game against Nebraska. He scored four touchdowns on long runs as Illinois won, 24-7. A few weeks later he snaked 90 yards through the entire Northwestern team for another touchdown. When Walter Camp named his annual All-American team, the Galloping Ghost was one of the two halfbacks. It was the first of three times Red would be on the All-America team.

In 1923 and 1924 Illinois lost only one game and tied one. Their greatest victory was the upset of Michigan, in which Red ran or passed for all six touchdowns. In 1925, most of his stars now graduated, coach Bob Zuppke moved Grange from left halfback to quarterback, where he could call the plays as well as run and pass. Midway through the season, once-beaten Illinois came east to play unbeaten Pennsylvania. Although everyone in the country had read about Grange, Easterners still believed that the powerful Eastern teams were superior to those in the Midwest. The Illinois–Pennsylvania game was to be the test of Eastern supremacy.

In the second half, Illinois was ahead by a narrow margin. With his team just past midfield, Grange called for the Illinois "flea flicker" play. Grange knelt, as if to

Although he weighed only 170 pounds, the Galloping Ghost has become a legend in a big man's game.

hold the ball for a field-goal attempt. But the pass from center went directly to the kicker, who threw a short pass to end Chuck Kassel. Kassel lateraled the ball to Grange, who shot by the startled Pennsylvania defense and ran 40 yards for a touchdown. Illinois scored again and finally won, 24–2.

As soon as he had finished his senior season at Illinois, Grange joined the Chicago Bears of the National Football League. Between Thanksgiving and Christmas, he toured the whole United States with the Bears, sometimes playing as many as four regular and all-star teams a week. He earned $100,000 and became the first superstar of professional football. Many believe that Grange was responsible for the growth of pro football from a local sport to a national pastime.

From 1926 through 1928 he played with the New York Yankees, members of a maverick league which he and his business manager had organized. Late in 1928 he hurt his knee, and never regained his mastery of broken-field running. But running mostly straight ahead, he still could outrun most defense men. On defense, he picked off passes with the deftness of a pickpocket.

In 1929 he returned to the Bears and played well enough in 1931 to make the first All-Pro team. In 1932 he scored nine touchdowns, leading the Bears to the NFL championship. On January 27, 1935, playing for the Bears against a Los Angeles all-star team, he broke loose on a 50-yard run. But as he crossed the 20, his legs iron-heavy, a 230-pound guard collared him from behind. Grange got up, looked at the lumbering man who had outrun him, and walked off the field. He never played again.

From 1922 until the mid-thirties, Grange had terrorized his opponents and excited his fans as few football stars ever have. Since his day there have been many great open-field runners, but for those who saw Red Grange run, there can be only one Galloping Ghost.

A dour-faced Grange rests on the bench while his own team, the New York Yankees, defeats the Philadelphia Quakers in 1926.

Ben Hogan

It was early in the morning and the fog lay heavy over the broad, peach-colored plains of West Texas. Ben Hogan, the greatest professional golfer of his age, was driving his Cadillac eastward through the fog. He had just completed a tournament in Arizona, and was heading home to Fort Worth with his wife, Valerie. Suddenly on that empty plain, just outside the small town of Van Horn, the lights of a bus glared through the windshield of the automobile, and in an instant there was the terrible, grinding noise of a head-on collision.

In the gnarled wreckage on that February morning in 1949, Hogan lay across the front seat unconscious and battered. He had a double fracture of the pelvis, a fractured collarbone, a broken left ankle and numerous lesser injuries. By all rights he should not have been alive.

Only a few hours later the news was flashed around the world that Ben Hogan, the U. S. Open champion and the PGA champion, five times the leading money winner of pro golf, was in grave condition, in a hospital in El Paso, Texas. Even if Hogan pulled through, he would surely never be able to play winning golf again. It seemed that this was the end of his career.

But it was only the beginning. Out of that near-fatal accident came a new Ben Hogan who, in one of the sports world's most brilliant comebacks, would win more important championships than he had ever won before.

First, Hogan had to learn to walk again. Next, he had to learn to swing a golf club again. All of this he did. And exactly eleven months after the car wreck, he turned up at the Los Angeles Open, one of the oldest tournaments on the professional circuit. With the fierce determination that had always characterized his play, Hogan was back. Ben trudged slowly over the fairways of that tournament and managed to tie Sam Snead for first place after 72 holes. The fact that he lost the play-off the next day didn't matter. Hogan was back.

Hogan was an entirely different man, not only in appearance, but in personality as well. He was mellower and heftier, no longer the grim Bantam Ben of the 1930s and 1940s. He had been quiet and icy and at times even waspish with his closest friends. But now he was more confident and dignified. He was stronger through the arms and shoulders, and his golf swing seemed to be more complete.

The Hogan comeback was not complete, however, until June of 1950 at the Merion Golf Club in Ardmore, Pennsylvania. The pros were gathered there for the U. S. Open championship, the biggest and most important championship in golf. Only six months had elapsed since Hogan had played in Los Angeles.

The U. S. Open was then the tournament in which a pro could win more money and prestige than in any other. The Merion course, already one of the toughest in the country, was carefully manicured for the occasion. Fairways were made narrower, and greens were so slick that putting on them was tricky. The rough bordering the fairways was allowed to grow very high and thick, and shots into it became far more difficult to play.

Hogan stayed in contention through the first two 18-hole rounds. The last 36 holes on Saturday would determine the winner. The big question was whether Hogan, limping and tired, could withstand two full

Ben Hogan tees off during his sensational comeback in the 1950 Los Angeles Open.

rounds in a single day under the pressure of the tournament. As he played, huge galleries lined every fairway to root for the little man in the white cap. Finally, there were three holes remaining—the three toughest on the course. Hogan needed a par on one of them, to tie for the championship. If he could par two of them, he could win.

But he went one over par on the sixteenth and seventeenth. As he stood on the eighteenth tee, he needed a par four to tie. The crowd fell silent as Hogan lashed a tee shot nearly 250 yards over a gully. Now everything hinged on the next shot.

It was a 2-iron shot to the green. The ball would have to travel 180 yards to the small green. Then he would have two putts for his par four. Hogan made one of the finest shots of his career—the ball blazed toward the flag and came to rest on the green about 25 feet from the hole. His sec-

ond putt dropped into the hole, making a play-off for the championship necessary. The next day, he easily defeated Lloyd Mangrum and George Fazio.

The following year he captured both the Masters championship in Augusta, Georgia, and the U. S. Open championship. This time he won the Open at Oakland Hills in Detroit, a course labeled "The Monster" by golfers. But on the last 18 holes of the tournament, Hogan shot an amazing 67, three under par. He later called it the "finest single round I have ever played." He said that if he had to play Oakland Hills for a living he would look for other work. But he felt a great sense of accomplishment, telling the writers and photographers who greeted him on the final green, "I finally brought the Monster to its knees."

Hogan's epic season was 1953, a year in which he crowned his career with the most sensational accomplishment since Bobby

Hogan proudly accepts the winner's trophy in the 1950 National Open. Lloyd Mangrum (right), the runner-up, applauds Hogan's victory.

In this putt, Ben reveals the putting form that made him a champion.

Jones's Grand Slam of 1930. Hogan won the Open for a fourth time—matching the record of Bobby Jones and Willie Anderson. He also won the Masters for a second time, and won the British Open in his only attempt to seek the title. It was a Triple Crown. When he returned from the British Open at Carnoustie, Scotland, in July, "the Wee Ice Mon," as the Scots called him, received a tickertape parade in New York City.

Hogan had come back to dominate golf once again. The New York parade was a fitting tribute. In all, Hogan won more than seventy tournaments in pro golf. His nine major victories (four U. S. Opens, two Masters, two PGAs, one British Open) placed him third behind only Jones and Walter Hagen, and made him a member of golf's Hall of Fame.

Although Hogan always argued that golf was a game that could never be conquered, he came closer than anyone to doing it.

63

Rafer Johnson

Darkness had fallen on Rome's Stadio Olympico. In the background burned the eternal Olympic torch, casting its light on two solitary figures running, one behind the other, around the darkened track.

Only a few spectators remained in the stands, for it was nearly midnight. The silence was broken only by the rhythmic footsteps of the two runners. One was C. K. Yang, a student at the University of California, Los Angeles, representing Nationalist China; the other was Rafer Johnson, another UCLA student, representing the United States.

Yang was leading by a few yards but Johnson was matching him stride for stride. When Yang quickened his pace, Johnson quickened his and when Yang slackened, so did Johnson.

They were competing in the 1500-meter run, the last event of the decathlon. In the past two days, both of them had tried their skill at the 100-meter dash, the broad jump, the shot-put, the high jump, the 400-meter run, the 110-meter hurdles, the discus, the pole vault and the javelin. The winner would be the man who had shown himself to be the best all-round athlete by winning the most points.

Going into the 1500 meters (slightly more than a mile), Johnson had a small 67-point lead over his friend Yang. But Yang was better equipped for the long race. In fact Johnson had almost conceded the race to Yang, but he had not conceded the gold medal. All he had to do was stay within ten seconds of Yang and the gold medal would be his. He had worked too hard and waited too long to fail now.

Four years earlier, Rafer Johnson had gone to the Olympic Games in Melbourne, heavily favored to win the decathlon, but he hadn't won. In the Olympic trials, he had injured his knee. And on the first day of the competition, he had torn a muscle in his abdomen in the high jump. Although he continued to compete, the pain in his stomach and his bad knee hampered him and he finished an unsatisfactory second. This time he would not be content with anything less than a gold medal.

Rafer Johnson was born on August 18, 1934, in Hillsboro, Texas, a small town south of Dallas. He was the second of six children. The Johnsons were familiar with segregation, discrimination and poverty in

Johnson (right) strains to keep up with C. K. Yang in the 1500 meter run, the last event in the 1960 Olympic decathlon.

Texas. When Rafer was eleven years old, his father moved the family to Kingsburg, a small town in central California. Segregation and discrimination were left behind, but poverty made the journey with them.

The Johnsons lived for a year in a boxcar with a tattered curtain for a room divider until Edward Fishel, owner of a small animal-feed processing plant, took an interest in them. He hired Rafer's father as a handyman and his mother as a domestic and he moved the family into a small house.

Rafer was a quiet, shy boy, but he soon learned to use athletics as his means of expression. As a halfback, he led Kingsburg High to three football championships. He averaged 17 points a game in basketball and batted .400 in baseball. But his greatest love was track and field. He specialized in no single event but excelled in them all.

In his junior year, Rafer's coach, Murl Dodson, took him to the nearby town of Tulare to watch the famous young Californian, Bob Mathias, who had won the 1948 and 1952 Olympic decathlons. On the ride back to Kingsburg, Rafer was quiet. Finally, he said, "You know, coach, I could have beaten most of those guys in that meet."

Rafer began training for the decathlon immediately. Four weeks later, he won the California Junior AAU decathlon championship. He repeated this triumph the following year. He then entered the National AAU decathlon in Atlantic City, New Jersey, and finished third. But third wasn't good enough for Rafer. Only winning satisfied him.

Rafer accepted an athletic scholarship to

Rafer practices the high hurdles.

65

UCLA. Football fans hoped that he would give UCLA's football fortunes a lift. But he passed up football to concentrate on track. He won the decathlon at the 1955 Pan-American Games in Mexico City and later returned to Kingsburg to compete in a special decathlon there. With friends and family looking on, Rafer scored 7,985 points to break Mathias' world record by 98 points.

He did not have the record for long. The Russian, Vasily Kuznetsov, compiled a total of 8,014 points a few months later. The track world looked forward to the meeting of Johnson and Kuznetsov in the United States–Russia meet in Moscow in the summer of 1958.

When the final event had been run at Moscow, Rafer Johnson was declared the winner with a record-breaking 8,302 points. Proudly the young American climbed the podium and stood tall while 30,000 Russians in Lenin Stadium gave him a standing ovation. Vasily Kuznetsov, the beaten hero, placed a congratulatory kiss on the cheek of his conqueror. The next day, a Moscow paper said, "His performance will dignify the history of world athletics for a long time to come."

But again his record did not last. In 1959 Kuznetsov topped it with 8,357 points while Rafer lay in a hospital bed. Johnson had severely injured his back in an automobile accident. For nineteen months he could neither compete nor train. Finally, in February of 1960, he resumed training and in July of that year, he competed in the National AAU decathlon at Eugene, Oregon.

After eight events, Rafer held a commanding lead over his old rivals, Kuznetsov and Yang, and in the ninth event, the javelin, he knew he could regain his world record. As soon as he had released the spear, he was certain that he had done it: once again the record was his. He leaped into the air

and raced down the field to retrieve his javelin.

Rafer Johnson had come back, but his job was only half complete. It would not be finished until the Olympic gold medal was placed around his neck. He was the decathlon record holder; he had been elected president of the UCLA student body; and he had been selected to carry the American flag in the opening ceremonies of the 1960 Olympics, the first Negro to be so honored. But the gold medal still had to be won.

He and Yang were 300 yards from the finish line. They had run almost a mile and now Yang picked up the pace, trying to increase his lead. But Johnson stayed close.

"I could see him behind me at the turns," Yang said later. "I could see his dark form and I knew he would never let go of me unless he collapsed."

Johnson did collapse after he had crossed the finish line practically at Yang's heels. He collapsed into the arms of his Chinese friend, pain and exhaustion written on his face. It was over, and he had won his gold medal.

Vasily Kuznetsov, Russian decathlon champ, congratulates Johnson for winning the decathlon in the 1958 U.S.–Russia competition.

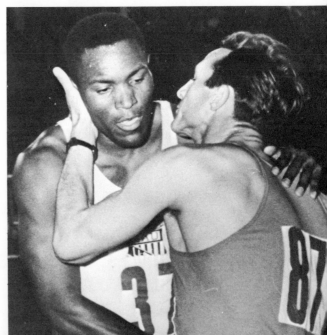

66

Bobby Jones

Outside his family's summer home near Atlanta, Georgia, a five-year-old boy was swinging a sawed-off golf club at some battered golf balls. This little fellow who was whacking the ball along a road that bordered the East Lake Golf Club was a lawyer's son named Bobby Jones, Jr.

Bobby's parents had taken up golf at East Lake, and soon he was trailing them around the course, swinging the club as he went. Then the boy began playing himself. He took to the game from the start. He won his first championship in 1912 at the age of nine, beating a 16-year-old opponent in the final round of a junior tournament. He broke 80 before his twelfth birthday. When he was fourteen he won the Georgia amateur title and set out in quest of his first major championship—the National Amateur.

In the summer of 1916, the Amateur was held at the Merion Cricket Club near Philadelphia. To everyone's amazement, the boy from Atlanta led the field in the first qualifying round by whipping around the course with a 74. In the second round he slumped to an 89, but his total still qualified him for the tournament.

In the next round Bobby polished off former champion Eben Byers. Then he beat Pennsylvania champion Frank Dyer. In the third round, he faced Bob Gardner, the defending champion. The contrast between the two players was startling. Gardner was a former Yale athlete, who had once set a world's record in the pole vault. He was a

A handsome, clean-cut young man, Bobby helped make golf a popular sport in America.

Jones blasts out of a bunker at the 1930 British Open where he began his famous sweep of golf prizes.

handsome, superbly built six-footer. His opponent was a pudgy fifteen-year-old, who stood 5 feet 4 inches, tugged frequently at his first pair of long pants, and clumped down the fairways in a pair of hand-me-down Army shoes into which he had screwed some spikes.

At the halfway mark in the 36-hole match, Jones was one up. Sports writers, among them the famous Grantland Rice, came flocking from the other matches to watch the battle between the champion and the boy wonder. With the help of three fantastic recovery shots, Gardner won. But Bobby Jones had definitely arrived on the scene.

Gradually the Jones boy grew up. He stopped throwing clubs when things went wrong with his game. Not content to let golf rule his life, he completed his education at Georgia Tech and Harvard Law School. And he perfected a smooth, strong golf swing that could have been used as a copybook example.

At the Inwood Country Club on Long Island in 1923, Jones defeated Bobby Cruickshank in a play-off to win the National Open. He had won his first major title at the age of twenty and for the next seven years there was no holding him. Soon everyone who looked at sports pages recognized his picture. He was a stocky, smiling, square-faced young man who parted his hair in the center and played golf in knickers. He became a star in the Golden Age of Sports (the 1920s) along with Babe Ruth, Jack Dempsey and Red Grange.

Jones remained an amateur in a game that was led by professionals. But he was just too good for his competition, pro or amateur. His game had no flaws. After he shot an amazing 66 in a tournament at his old home course, sports writer Kerr Petrie wrote: "They wound up the Mechanical Man of Golf yesterday and sent him clicking around the East Lake course."

The climax came in 1930. Jones started the year by winning the British Amateur for the first time. Next he won the British Open. Back home, Bobby stood off the field in the final round of the U. S. Open at Interlachen in Minneapolis.

That left the National Amateur, which once again was being played at Merion, where he had played his first National tournament fourteen years earlier. On the twenty-ninth hole of the final-round match, Gene Homans needed a long putt to have a chance of tying Jones. When it failed to drop, Homans strode across the green and shook hands with the man who had done the impossible. By winning the Amateur, Jones had completed an unparalleled Grand Slam. He had won the amateur and open championships of the United States and England in the same year. That gave him a career total of thirteen major championships, a record still unmatched in 1966.

Jones was then only twenty-eight years old, but he had no more worlds to conquer. He gave up his amateur standing to make a series of instructional movies on golf. But though he was technically a pro, Bobby wanted no more big-time competition. He said in his retirement announcement: "Fourteen years of intensive tournament play in this country and abroad have given me about all I want in the way of hard work in the game."

When he was forty-six Jones was stricken with a crippling nerve affliction that eventually put him in a wheelchair. He could no longer play golf, even for the fun of it. Fortunately, however, he was able to remain close to golf and golfers through his interest in the Augusta National Golf Club in Georgia. He and some friends founded the club in 1930 and instituted the Masters tournament, which has gradually acquired more prestige than any other golf event in this country except the National Open. The Masters remains as a memorial to Bobby Jones, who died in 1971 at the age of 69.

Jones hits iron shot in the 1930 U.S. Open, continuing his Grand Slam of golf.

Sandy Koufax

Sandy Koufax ripped his spikes angrily across the mound, a grim frown on his face. The catcher was walking slowly toward him. This was a spring exhibition game in 1961 between a Dodger "B" team and White Sox rookies. For Sandy Koufax, Los Angeles Dodger left-hander, this game would become the most meaningful one of his career.

Around him, at each base, were White Sox runners. There was no one out, and the bases were loaded. Koufax had been in this situation before: he had filled the bases dozens of times in his six-year career. He was the fastest pitcher in baseball, but he was "high wild" they said in the dugouts, meaning he threw high sailing pitches that batters took for walks. For six years Sandy had lost as often as he had won.

The evening before the "B" game with the White Sox, Sandy had been talking with catcher Norm Sherry. "Look," said Sherry, "if you get behind on a hitter, do me a favor.

Sandy's blazing fast ball requires all of his strength and concentration.

Don't force your fastball. That's when you get real wild. Throw it easy." Koufax had been doubtful—this was the hundredth theory he'd heard about his wildness—but he agreed to try. Now he was angry at himself, and Sherry had come out to talk to him. "Remember what I told you," Sherry said. "Just throw easy."

"I guess I have nothing to lose," said Sandy.

He began to throw his fastball with an easy motion, and one–two–three the batters went down without scoring a run. Later Koufax remembered that inning and said: "I'll never forget it. Then and there I realized that there's no need to throw as hard as I can. I found out if I take it easy and throw naturally, the ball goes just as fast."

Almost overnight the scatter-armed pitcher had found control. In 1961 he won 18 and lost 13 games, and led the league in strikeouts; a year earlier, he had only 8 wins. In the next few years he pitched the Dodgers to two world championships. "If there was ever a better pitcher," says Walter Alston, Dodger manager, "it was before my time."

Koufax was born in 1935, and grew up in Brooklyn, where kids play mostly on sidewalks and paved playgrounds. Since the pavement is too hard for baseball, Sandy grew up playing basketball. When he was eleven years old, he and his pals played in the Jewish Community House league, and Sandy made the all-midget team.

Later, some of his friends joined the Parkviews, an amateur sandlot baseball team, and Sandy tagged along. One day, when he was whipping the ball around the infield, the Parkview manager said to him: "With that kind of arm, you should be a pitcher."

Sandy gave it a try, and with the Koufax fastball humming by batters, Parkview won

the league title. Big league scouts came to see him, but Sandy was only half-interested. He had already received a basketball scholarship from the University of Cincinnati. He enrolled at Cincinnati in the fall of 1953. As a freshman, he averaged 10 points a game, but when the Brooklyn Dodgers offered him a $14,000 bonus to sign a baseball contract, Sandy couldn't say no.

In 1955 he was in a Dodger uniform at Ebbets Field. In his second big league start he shut out the Reds, yielding only two hits.

"It was wonderful when it happened," Sandy remembers. "But as I look back at it now, that game may have hurt me more than it helped. I threw real hard in the game, and it worked. . . . It took me a long time to learn that it was wrong."

After that exhibition game in 1961 he began to throw his fast one with that easy motion. One of Sandy's greatest achievements took place on the night of September 9, 1965, when he faced the Chicago Cubs at Dodger Stadium. Inning after inning,

Holding up a ball for each of his four no-hitters, Sandy beams after pitching his perfect game against the Cubs on September 9, 1965.

three Cubs came up, three Cubs went down. Dodger batters were just as helpless against the Cubs' Bobby Hendley, but in the fifth they got an unearned run. In the seventh they got a hit, the first and only one they would get.

With the Dodgers ahead, 1–0, in the eighth, Koufax struck out Ron Santo, then Ernie Banks, then Byron Browne. In the ninth, the crowd of 29,000 cheering on every pitch, he struck out Chris Krug, then Joey Amalfitano. Up came Harvey Kuenn, a great hitter, and down he went, Sandy's fourteenth strikeout.

Koufax ran off the mound, jubilant, and his teammates hugged him. He was the first pitcher ever to pitch four no-hitters. And this one was a perfect game: 27 men up, 27 men down, no walks, no hits, no errors.

Sandy's success, however, was accompanied by painful and potentially disabling ailments. In 1962 a circulatory blockage cut off the flow of blood to a finger on his pitching hand. In 1965 arthritis attacked his elbow. Following the 1966 World Series, this crippling disease finally forced the $125,000-a-year hurler to retire.

But Sandy seldom complained. Despite all his troubles, he spent the years since 1962 collecting pitching records. In 1963 he pitched the Dodgers to the pennant and helped mop up the New York Yankees in the World Series in four straight games. He became one of the few pitchers ever to win the Most Valuable Player award. In 1964, he compiled the lowest earned-run average (1.74) in the National League since 1933. And in 1965, he set a new major league record by striking out 382 batters in one season, thereby becoming the fourth pitcher in modern times to strike out more than 300 in a season. He also won 26 games and achieved the league's lowest earned-run average for the fourth straight year.

He has had bad years as well as good, and so is a realist. In the second game of the 1965 World Series he was beaten by the Twins' Jim Kaat. When a reporter asked him if his control had been bad, he replied, "I pitched a good game, but Kaat pitched a better game, and that's all there is to that."

In the fifth and seventh games of the Series, Sandy faced Kaat again. Both times, he shut out the Twins and struck out 10 men. In three starts, he had struck out 29 men in 24 innings and given up only two runs. It added up to one of the most superlative Series in pitching history and provided additional testimony for Koufax as the greatest left-hander ever.

Koufax ponders his next pitch against the Twins in the second game of the 1965 World Series. He lost this game but won two others.

Jack Kramer

The boy was heartbroken. He loved to play football and now his parents had told him he couldn't play it any more. A few weeks earlier he had mashed his nose in a scrimmage and today he had walked off the field with separated ribs. Try another sport, his father said. Try tennis.

Tennis? Not for Jack Kramer. He loved body combat. He loved to block and to tackle and to plunge into the thick of a tough, strong line. He couldn't be happy simply patting a ball across a net. But his parents insisted.

Jack played his first game of tennis against his father in Las Vegas, Nevada. Soon afterward, the Kramers moved to San Bernardino, California. There father and son spent hours on the tennis courts smashing the ball at each other, running full fury, neither letting up. Jack hated to lose in these matches, but often he did. One day, after a resounding loss, he walked off the court and refused to play an extra set. His father, who hated sore losers, decided never to play with him again.

But Mr. Kramer soon changed his mind. For Jack began to want to play against anyone at any time. He took his racket to school with him. He skipped meals to play sets. He loved the challenge of standing up to a whizzing serve and trying to smash it back. He liked to wallop his own serve past a quick, poised opponent and to stand on a court, mouth parched, body exhausted, trying to muster the energy for one more attack.

Kramer reaches high to return the ball to Bobby Riggs in a 1947 match.

73

Jack began to dream of becoming a tennis champion. He took lessons from Dick Skene, a professional player. He paid for them out of his own savings. In time Jack left Skene and began taking lessons from Perry Jones. Perry said that if Jack was to become a champion, he would have to play champions. When Jack was fifteen years old, Perry arranged a match for him with Alice Marble, the United States and British women's champion. Jack beat her. Jones entered him in the national boys' tournament. Jack won the championship.

Two years later Kramer went to Forest Hills, New York, to play in the U. S. National men's tournament. He was a happy, friendly seventeen-year-old, with a big grin and a warm greeting for everyone. One of Jack's friends, Frankie Kovacs, loved to eat. For days he and Jack ate almost nothing but spaghetti and hot dogs. Sick to his stomach, Jack was knocked out of the tournament in an early round.

The next year Jack played on the United States Davis Cup squad. At eighteen, he was one of the youngest players ever to earn such an honor. But he was unusual for his age. When he stretched to the tip of his toes and unleashed a serve with all his strength, it was as fast as anyone's since Bill Tilden, the great star of the 1920s. When he raced across the court, shot out a long arm and whipped in a backhand shot, people compared him with Don Budge, another Californian, who had dominated tennis in the mid-30s.

Kramer, however, had a talent all his own. At nineteen he won ten straight tournaments but, because of an appendicitis attack, he did not play in the U. S. Nationals. In 1943, at twenty, he won another string of tournaments, but, assaulted by ptomaine poisoning, lost the final match in the Nationals.

By then the United States was fighting in World War II. Jack joined the Coast Guard and did not return to tennis until 1946. In his first big tournament, the Wimbledon in London, he was beaten by Jaroslav Drobny. Newspapermen said Jack had lost because of a badly blistered hand. "Nonsense," said Jack. "The injury didn't beat me. Drobny did."

Jack always snubbed excuses and spoke his mind. He was a captivating hero—outspoken, tall, handsome and dedicated to power on the tennis court. People called him Big Jake and knew that no match he played in would be dull.

He went to Forest Hills in September, 1946, and finally won the U. S. Nationals. He went to Australia in December and, with Ted Schroeder, won back the Davis Cup for the United States. He returned to Wimbledon in 1947 and won the British championship.

Jack was clearly the best of all amateur players, and tennis fans began to wonder

Kramer now arranges professional tennis matches all over the world.

74

how he would do against the professional champ, Bobby Riggs. "I can beat Jack Kramer on grass, on clay, on cement or indoors," Riggs said. And Jack said, "I figure I can beat any defensive player in the world and Riggs, by his own admission, is a defensive player."

Riggs offered Jack a big contract to turn professional and Jack, who had never had much money, was eager to take it. But first he wanted to win the U. S. Nationals again.

Jack swept through the Nationals to the finals. But in the final match, he was suddenly being beaten by Frank Parker, a shrewd, soft-hitting 31-year-old. Aware that he could not overpower Big Jake, Frank was outsmarting him. When Jack charged the net, Parker lobbed the ball over his head. When Jack stayed back at the baseline, Parker dropped the ball inches over the net. Parker won the first set, 6–4, and the second, 6–2. One more set and Parker, not Jack Kramer, would be the champ.

Jack suddenly switched tactics. He stopped smashing the ball and began tapping it. Though he loved to attack and please the fans with his eye-popping power, Big Jake could play a defensive game, too. Outmaneuvering Parker, he won the third set, 6–1, and the fourth, 6–0. In the fifth set, with Parker exhausted, Jack switched back to his power game. He rocketed serves, slammed ground strokes, charged the net and smashed overhead shots. He won 6–3.

Then Jack turned professional and toured the country with Bobby Riggs. They played each other more than 100 times. Jack lived up to his boast, winning more than three-quarters of the matches. "He was a merciless competitor," Riggs said years later. "Even when he had huge leads in our series, Jack was sore when he lost. He fought from the first match to the last."

Three all-time great pros—(left to right) Jack Kramer, Bobby Riggs and Frank Parker.

As pro champ, Kramer met a new challenger each year. He turned back each one. First he beat Pancho Gonzales, then Pancho Segura and then Frank Sedgman. In 1954 he retired from play to become a tennis promoter and a businessman.

By 1965 Kramer was a wealthy man, but he had not lost interest in tennis. He coached U. S. Davis Cup players and young players at clinics. Worried about tennis' loss of appeal in the United States, he continually offered ideas to help revive the sport. His ideas often bucked tennis tradition but, typically, Big Jake never drew back under criticism. He favored open tennis, tournaments in which pros and amateurs would play each other. He suggested rules changes. He said that too many youngsters considered tennis a "sissy" sport and that tennis people ought to work hard to show them how wrong they were.

Kramer knew that throughout the United States there were many potential tennis champions who might never take up the sport because they didn't know how tough and challenging it really was. He had nearly been one of those himself.

Joe Louis

Louis lands the decisive punch against Max Schmeling in their 1938 title fight.

After school each afternoon, Joe Louis Barrow and Freddie Guinyard would run to an ice plant near their homes in Detroit and climb on the truck that delivered ice. When the truck arrived at a delivery point, Joe would hop off and Freddie would slide a 50-pound block of ice on Joe's back. "Okay, Joe," Freddie would say, "you take up the ice and I'll watch the truck."

Then Joe would carry the ice up four flights of stairs to someone's icebox. When he came down, Freddie would put another block on Joe's shoulders and Joe would carry it up to someone else's icebox.

Carrying all that ice helped build Joe Louis Barrow into a big, strong, six-foot, 200-pound man. When he took up boxing, he dropped his last name and became Joe Louis. For twelve years, longer than anyone before or since, Joe Louis was world heavyweight champion. He had 71 fights, won 54 by knockout, lost only three— two of them when, old and tired, he attempted a comeback.

Of all his fights, none was more dramatic than his second fight with Germany's Max Schmeling in 1938. Two years earlier Schmeling had knocked out Louis. Adolf Hitler, the German dictator, used Max as proof for propaganda purposes that Germans were "the master race."

Soon after his fight with Schmeling, Louis—a Negro—became the heavyweight champion of the world. Hitler wanted Schmeling to take that title from Louis to prove that Germans were superior. Seventy thousand fans packed Yankee Stadium for the match and millions around the world listened on radio, for this was a fight with world-wide political overtones.

At the bell, the scowling Schmeling moved out cautiously, away from Louis' powerful right. Then suddenly, Louis' left hook raked Max's face, another left caught his chin, a third smashed his ribs. Then Joe caught Schmeling with a right flush on the chin. Schmeling crashed against the ropes, and Louis continued to hammer him, each punch straightening the sagging German.

Schmeling went down. He got up at the count of 3, and Louis swarmed over him again. A right, a left, and down went

Joe throws a hard left at Billy Conn in 1941.

Louis winds up for a right against Joe Walcott in 1948.

Schmeling again. He got up and Louis knocked him down a third time. This time, Schmeling did not get up. The referee counted 10, and the fight was over—in two minutes and four seconds of the first round.

The son of a tenant farmer, Joe Louis was born in his father's shack on May 13, 1914. When he was twelve, his family, including his parents and thirteen children, moved to Detroit. Joe went to school in Detroit but since he could barely read and write, he was placed in a lower grade among much younger children. He was

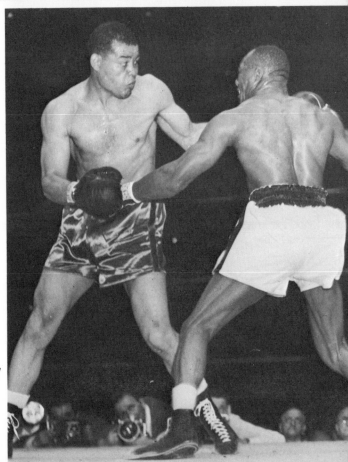

77

embarrassed, and he learned slowly.

But he did make friends with Freddie Guinyard, who got him the job delivering ice. In 1932, as a strapping eighteen-year-old Joe learned that an amateur boxing club was paying fighters with food. With hungry brothers and sisters at home, Joe signed up for a fight.

Knowing almost nothing about boxing, Joe was knocked down seven times in his first two rounds. He went home aching, and swore never to box again. He gave his mother the seven dollars in food that he had received. A little later he quit school and took a factory job.

Joe soon met Holman Williams, a professional boxer, who taught him some basic boxing moves. Williams talked Joe into entering the 1933 Golden Gloves. And Joe, now that he knew how to block a punch, won the Golden Gloves light-heavyweight title in 1933 and again in 1934. His Golden Gloves victories impressed John Roxborough, a Detroit lawyer, who signed him to a professional contract and then turned Joe over to Jack Blackburn, a skilled trainer.

Joe learned slowly but well. He won his first professional fight on July 4, 1934, on a one-round knockout. He won his next by KO, then another. Soon sports writers were calling him the "Brown Bomber," a nickname that stayed with him until the end of his career.

One of his victims was carted to a hospital with a concussion. "I am sorry that happened," Louis said. "But they come to beat me up. I have to go back at them the same way."

Then Joe came to New York and knocked out gigantic Primo Carnera, the former heavyweight champion. His income began to rise and soon he was earning $250,000 a fight. He spent nearly every-

thing he owned on fancy clothes, big cars and bad investments. If a friend needed a thousand dollars, Joe gave it to him. "They must need it if they ask for it," he would say.

In 1937 he beat Jim Braddock to win the heavyweight championship. During the next five years he defended the title twenty-one times, fighting as often as five times a year. Only two challengers went the full 15 rounds against him.

Then World War II began. He joined the army, visiting all the battle zones, entertaining troops with boxing exhibitions. In 1946, out of the army, he knocked out Billy Conn in the eighth round.

His career took a fast plunge, however, when he took on Jersey Joe Walcott in 1947. Walcott knocked Joe down twice, but Louis got the decision. Boxing fans said Joe was washed up and that Walcott should be the new champ. A year later Louis met Walcott again and knocked him out. This time the fans were satisfied. On March 1, 1949, Louis retired as champion.

But with the government pressing him for money for back taxes, he attempted a comeback in 1950. The new heavyweight champion, Ezzard Charles, beat him easily in a fifteen-round decision. After the fight, Joe was led out of Yankee Stadium. Still Joe kept fighting, until powerful Rocky Marciano ended his boxing career in 1951, knocking him out in the fourth round.

Louis earned and lost four and a half million dollars during his career. Today he earns enough in various public relations jobs to live comfortably in homes in New York and Los Angeles. Although the "big money" is gone, Joe Louis knows he has something no one can take from him: his record. Of all the great heavyweights, no one fought and won as often in defense of his title. This is a record that money can't buy.

Sid Luckman

They were handing over Sid Luckman's quarterback job to young Johnny Lujack during the 1950 season. But one Sunday, as Sid pulled on the orange-and-black jersey of the Chicago Bears, he suddenly straightened up: "I've got to see if I can still move the team," he said to himself.

Sid walked over to George Halas. "Coach," Luckman said softly, "I'd like to play today." Halas, knowing 34-year-old Sid was recuperating from a minor operation and that this would be his last season, nodded his agreement. He decided to start him against Detroit that day.

On his second play, Sid got hit from the blind side as he cocked his arm to pass. The ball squirted loose. Detroit recovered it and scored almost immediately. Luckman, head down, ran to the bench. His home fans were booing, and he felt like hiding under his blanket. Then Halas was standing there, his arm around Sid's shoul-

Sid Luckman, near the end of his career, shakes hands with his successor Johnny Lujack.

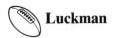

der. "Don't worry," he said. "You've done more than your share to make them happy."

Halas sent Luckman back in. Sid went back to pass again, and this time the old magic was still there. He delivered the ball on target, and Chicago scored a quick touchdown. Sid trotted off, head up. This time, the fans were standing for Luckman and cheering wildly.

Sid retired at the end of the season. But he had, indeed, given Chicago plenty to cheer about. He had passed, run and masterminded the Bears to four National Football League titles and five division championships.

Sid joined Halas' Bears in 1939 as a sturdy (six-foot, 200-pound) young man who could pass, run, punt, block and tackle. But he had never played quarterback in the new T formation—the position for which he had been drafted. During the 1920s and 1930s, nearly every college and professional team had used the single-wing formation. Luckman had been a single-wing tailback at Columbia University. But Halas was impressed with the flexibility of the new T formation that was being used by his friend Clark Shaughnessy at the University of Chicago. He wanted to use the T with the Bears and he wanted Luckman to be the first T quarterback.

So Luckman's rookie year became a postgraduate course to learn a thousand different assignments for every player in the line-up. Sid was to pioneer the way. "He learned those formations overnight," says Halas. "It astounded me."

Luckman also astounded NFL rivals in 1940. He quarterbacked his team into the championship game against Washington. Sid was matched against the Redskin's great passer, Sammy Baugh.

There was bad blood between the teams. The 'Skins had licked Chicago, 7–3, earlier

in the year, but the Bears had complained that an official's bad judgment had cost them the game. Washington called the Chicago players "crybabies" and said the Bears didn't have a second-half ball club.

On the second play from scrimmage, Luckman pitched out to Bill Osmanski. Osmanski circled left end and stormed 68 yards for a touchdown.

The next time the Bears got the ball, they marched 80 yards for another touchdown. Luckman went over from six inches out. The rout was on. The score was 28–0 at the half, and at the finish it was 73–0! Luckman had sat on the bench for the second half. The next day the New York *Times* recognized how Sid had destroyed Washington for good in the first half: "No field general ever called plays more artistically," the paper reported. "He was letter perfect."

That championship game revolutionized professional football. Within a few years, every team was using the T formation. Luckman's pioneer work as a T quarterback paved the way for modern football strategy —twenty-five years later, the T is still the pro formation.

Sid was a proud winner. In the 1944 game against the College All-Stars, the Bears gave up two quick touchdowns. "Where did you men get these uniforms— steal them?" raged Luckman in the huddle. "These uniforms will not be disgraced. I'll give you one more chance to throw your blocks. Otherwise I'm walking off this field."

The Bears won the game. Afterward, veteran lineman Bulldog Turner said, "He picked us up by our cleats and made us win this game."

Sid's most obvious contribution to the Bears' success was his passing. He was especially adept at arching long passes into his receivers' arms. He passed for 14,683 yards and 139 touchdowns in his 12-year career and the greatest single chunk of that came dramatically one day in 1943.

The Bears were playing the New York Giants in New York, where Luckman had grown up and gone to college. His friends arranged a "Sid Luckman Day" and gave him $2,000 in war bonds. Then the game began. Starting with a four-yard scoring pass to end Jim Benton, Luckman threw seven touchdown passes, setting an NFL

(Top) Luckman hands off to Bear halfback Hugh Gallaraneau. (Bottom) Sid keeps the ball and gains 10 yards against the Redskins.

record. The Bears won, 56–7.

After the game, Luckman went to the Giant dressing room and found New York coach Steve Owen. "Steve," he said, "I just want you to know I'm sorry we rolled up the score on you."

"You don't have to apologize," Owen replied. "I expect a team to play its best all the way. If it had to happen, I'm glad you were the one who did it."

Sid showed his football talents early. By his sophomore year at Erasmus Hall High School in Brooklyn, he had developed into a skilled runner, passer and kicker. He was soon the single-wing tailback and signal caller. In his senior year, Luckman was New York City's most sought-after school-boy football player. He had also won an award as the top student in his class.

During his three varsity years at Columbia University, Sid was a great triple-threat tailback. But the team lost consistently and Sid absorbed a constant battering: his nose was broken three times. He received no All-America recognition because of his team's poor record.

But Halas wanted Luckman more than any All-America. Sid was talented and he was tall. Halas wanted a big man for his T formation. "That advantage in height means an awful lot when you're under the center," he said. Halas bargained with Pittsburgh to be sure that he got Luckman first. Halas was successful and the Bears got their pioneering quarterback.

Chicago fans still compare each new quarterback with Sid Luckman. Billy Wade, who led Chicago to the title in 1963, says the comparison is flattering but unfair. "They never," says Wade, "will see anybody like him again." Even George Halas, who has been in football for more than fifty years, calls Luckman "the greatest play-caller I have ever seen."

81

Mickey Mantle

Baseball was Elven "Mutt" Mantle's first love. Whenever he could, at night and on weekends, he played semiprofessional baseball in his hometown of Commerce, Oklahoma. Mutt worked in the lead and zinc mines. But he was determined that there would be no life in the mines for his son, Mickey. Mutt dreamed of seeing his son in the major leagues. He decided even before the boy was born to name him Mickey after Mickey Cochrane, the great Detroit Tiger catcher.

When Mickey was only three, his father bought him a complete baseball uniform. And when he was five, Mutt began teaching him all he knew about baseball. Mickey was naturally right-handed, but his father thought he would have a tremendous advantage if he could hit both right- and left-handed. So he taught the boy to hit both ways.

In high school Mickey pitched and played the infield. He could throw hard and hit a ball a long way. But football was his game, and he dreamed of playing halfback for the University of Oklahoma. His love for football caused the first of a series of injuries that have plagued him ever since.

Mickey was the star halfback for Commerce High School. In one game, he was kicked in the left shin during a pile-up. He thought nothing of it and continued to play. But the next morning his ankle had ballooned to twice its normal size and turned purple. Mickey's father took him to an Oklahoma City hospital, where it was learned he had osteomyelitis, a rare bone disease. Osteomyelitis can be arrested, but it leaves the bones in a weakened condition and is the source of considerable pain.

For a time, doctors considered amputating Mickey's leg. Instead, they sent him home with a pair of crutches and ordered him to stay off the leg for six months. But being unable to compete was impossible for him, and less than two months later he tossed the crutches away and went back to football. The next spring he was playing baseball as usual.

One day Tom Greenwade, a Yankee scout, passed through Commerce on his way to look at a shortstop in Broken Arrow, Oklahoma. He stopped to watch a high-school game and spotted a blond boy with powerful arms and shoulders. He was impressed enough to offer Mantle a Yankee contract calling for $1500 in bonus and salary. Mickey signed, enabling the Yankees to accomplish one of the great steals in baseball.

After graduating from high school, Mickey was sent to the minor league team at Independence, Missouri. The following season he played for Joplin, Missouri, where he was, in his own words, "the worst shortstop in the world. I made over sixty errors, most of them on throws."

But the Yankees were impressed with Mickey's power and they invited him to spring training in 1951. They immediately moved him from shortstop to the outfield "for the protection of the fans in the first-base stands," Mickey says. He was still inexperienced, but when the Yankees brought him to New York to open the season Mickey felt he was on his way.

By June he had been sent back to the minors—to Kansas City, the best minor league team in the Yankee chain. He had

Mantle has shown the great advantages of switch-hitting. Here he is hitting home runs from both sides of the plate in the same game.

82

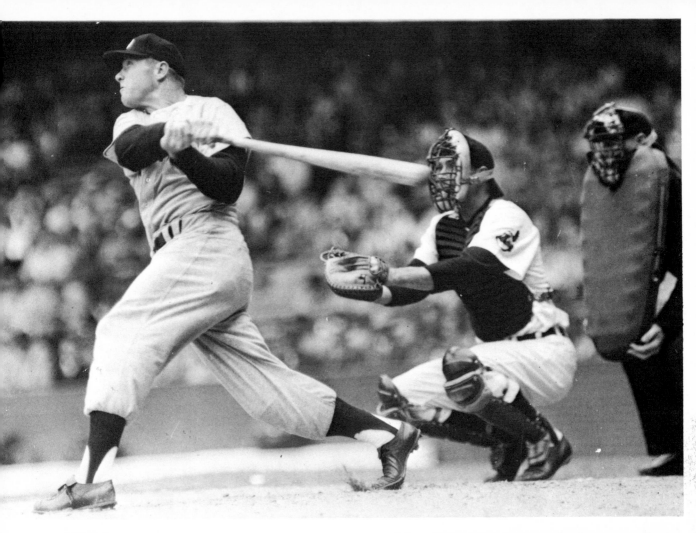

been striking out too much, and the Yankees figured a year in the minors would help. It didn't, though. At Kansas City, Mickey was worse than he had been with the Yankees. Then one day his father came to see him.

"My confidence was shot," Mickey recalls. "I started telling my father maybe I couldn't play ball. I figured he would say I was wrong, that I was a good player and everything would be all right. But he didn't say that. He said, 'Well, if that's all the guts you got, come on back and work in the mines with me. You don't belong in baseball.' Instead of sympathy, he kind of gave me a little needle."

Mickey responded to his father's prodding. He started to hit and within a month he was back with the Yankees, where he would gain the respect and admiration of everyone in and out of baseball.

Mutt Mantle came to New York in September of 1951 to see his son play in the World Series. Mickey got into two games, but in the second, while racing toward the centerfield wall for a fly ball, he caught his foot on a drainage spout and crumpled helplessly to the ground.

"I thought he had been shot," said center fielder Joe DiMaggio, who caught the ball over Mantle's prone body.

Mantle's injury was the most serious

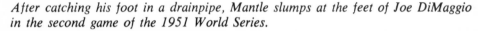

After catching his foot in a drainpipe, Mantle slumps at the feet of Joe DiMaggio in the second game of the 1951 World Series.

since the high-school football injury. It was only the first of many in his major league career. But for Mutt Mantle, Mickey's play proved that his hard work and determination had paid off. He did not live to see his son become the greatest switch hitter in baseball. But seeing his son in the 1951 World Series was the fulfillment of a dream.

In 1956, Mickey won the first of three American League Most Valuable Player awards. He batted .353 that year, had 130 RBI's and 52 home runs. He was just twenty-five, in the prime of his career, and he should have gone on to greater achievements, but he was hobbled by another long series of injuries.

Mickey had always been a better hitter right-handed than left. His average, right-handed, was .350, while his left-handed average was only .280. A few people believe that he might have been a .400 hitter if he had given up batting left-handed. But most observers agree that Mickey was a more dangerous hitter because of his ability to switch. He was able to take advantage of the higher probability that a right-hander will hit left-handed pitching and vice versa. Mutt Mantle knew baseball and Mickey's switch-hitting talent was regretted more by American League pitchers than by the Yankees.

When he retired in 1968, Mantle's statistical record was awesome: 536 home runs, 1,734 walks, 2,415 hits and 1,509 runs batted in. The statistics show only part of the way he dominated baseball during his career. From 1960 on, he did not play a single complete season without at least one serious injury. Yet his third Most Valuable Player award was won in 1963 and he was still pushing himself to the limit when he switched to first base in 1967.

His painful injuries did not keep Mickey from being a fearless baserunner. Here he slides into a second baseman to break up a double play.

Former pitcher Jim Bouton recalled what it was like playing as Mantle's teammate during those final years. "Even when he's not playing," Bouton said, "it's his voice you hear cheering you on from the dugout. He wants to win so badly. It makes you feel good being on the same team with him and having him cheer for you. It makes you want to go out and win for him."

Rocky Marciano

As a boy in Brockton, Massachusetts, Rocky Marciano's main interest was baseball. Because of his squat build and good throwing arm, he became a catcher. And whenever there was a baseball game, the chances were that Rocky would be in the thick of it. He played regularly for the Sons of Italy and for the Ward Two Social Club. Sometimes he would play ten or twelve games a week.

Rocky's father, Peter, worked in a Brockton shoe factory. Wages were low and there were six children to feed in the Marciano family. Rocky added his share to the family income by doing odd jobs. He worked as a gardener, in the shoe plant and in a candy factory. Then, during World War II, he went into the Army.

While he was stationed at Fort Lewis, Washington, Rocky rediscovered boxing. As a boy he had seen prize fights in Brockton, and his uncle John Piccento had bought him his first set of boxing gloves many years earlier. But he had never taken boxing very seriously. Now, weighing nearly 200 pounds and standing 5 feet, 11 inches tall, Rocky was challenged by the camp bully to enter the camp boxing tournament. Rocky entered it, beat the troublemaker and went on to win the title. He was later transferred to Europe with the 150th Combat Engineers, but he continued to box until he was discharged. All the time he was boxing, however, he still dreamed about a career as a professional baseball player.

In 1946, Ralph Wheeler, a Boston sports writer, arranged for Rocky to try out for the Chicago Cubs' minor league team in Fayetteville, North Carolina. Unfortunately his arm went dead within a week, and he was soon released. Rocky Marciano returned to Brockton a failure.

Back home, he got a job with the City of Brockton, clearing land for a housing project with pick and shovel. Then one day a lifelong friend, Allie Colombo, urged Rocky to compete in a local amateur boxing show. With Colombo serving as his chief cheerleader, Marciano soon fought his way to the Eastern finals of the Golden Gloves.

After the Golden Gloves success, Allie wrote to a few men in professional boxing. Al Weill, a shrewd manager who had handled a number of world champions, showed some interest in Rocky and agreed to look him over. After seeing him fight, Weill agreed to handle Rocky, and obtained the services of Charlie Goldman, one of the best fight trainers in the world.

For all his determination and courage, Rocky was in desperate need of a teacher. He used a mauling kind of style that had its advantages but would scarcely be successful on experienced pros. Charlie Goldman taught him to use his left hand more and showed him how to defend himself and conserve his energy.

Rocky was already twenty-four years old when he had his first professional fight. At that age, most good fighters are ready to fight for the championship. But Rocky had to put in four more years, fighting his way up the ranks. Finally, on September 22, 1952, he was set to box Jersey Joe Walcott for the heavyweight championship of the world.

The Marciano–Walcott title fight at Philadelphia's Municipal Stadium was one of the most exciting heavyweight bouts ever fought. In the very first round, Walcott knocked Marciano to his knees with a savage left hook. There were no more knockdowns through the twelfth round. By

Marciano shows his amazing power as he connects with fading ex-champion Joe Louis in 1951.

the end of the twelfth, a dangerous swelling had appeared under Rocky's eye. The canny Goldman was able to deflate it somewhat, but obviously Rocky would have to score a quick knockout before his eye swelled shut.

In the thirteenth round Walcott, his back to the ropes, threw a vicious right hand. But Rocky threw the same punch at the same time and his arrived first, crashing against the side of Walcott's jaw. Walcott fell first to his knees, then flat on his stomach. The fight was over.

Then everyone began climbing into the ring. Rocky's friends and neighbors, the kids he had grown up with and the people

In his last title defense, Marciano scores to the body of Archie Moore.

he had once worked for, were all there, trampling one another in their haste to get to the new champion.

Nobody ever beat Rocky Marciano. He defended his title six times and only one man, Ezzard Charles, stayed on his feet for fifteen rounds. In a return match, even Charles failed to finish. Rocky knocked him out in the eighth round. On April 27, 1956, seven months after knocking out Archie Moore, his last challenger, Rocky Marciano retired from boxing to devote more time to his wife, Barbara, and their children.

Marciano had fought 49 professional bouts, winning all of them—43 by knockout. He was named Fighter of the Year in 1952, '54 and '55, and earned one and a half million dollars in seven title fights. Wise business investments made Rocky a wealthy man, but he continued to attend the championship bouts, often as a radio commentator.

Marciano survived life's toughest battles

in and out of the ring. But on August 1, 1969—the day before his 46th birthday— he died in the crash of a private plane in Iowa. The champ finally was the victim of a force he could not control.

Rocky wins the championship as defending champion Joe Walcott slumps to the canvas unable to continue the fight.

88

Bob Mathias

Robert Bruce Mathias was fourteen years old and something definitely was wrong. He felt listless and tired and had frequent nose bleeds. His family physician found that he was anemic. Apparently the 5-foot, 10-inch youngster had grown faster than his body could stand. The doctor prescribed iron and liver pills and ordered Bob to take a nap every day after lunch. Bob did exactly as he was told, for the doctor was his father.

It wasn't easy for Bob to pamper himself, though, because he had always been exceptionally active. In athletics he was something of a child prodigy. When he was twelve years old he entered his first track meet. It was a grade-school competition and he won the high jump by jumping 5 feet, 6 inches. At dinner that night his brother Gene couldn't believe that Bob had jumped that high. Gene had competed in a high-school meet the same day, and there the winning high jump had been only 5 feet, 5 inches.

For the whole year, however, the most strenuous thing Bob was allowed to do was play the trumpet in the high-school band. Finally, when he was fifteen, his father called a halt to the naps. Bob celebrated by quickly establishing a reputation as the finest all-round athlete in his hometown of Tulare, California; in fact, in the whole San Joaquin Valley. In football he averaged nearly nine yards a carry and in basketball he averaged eighteen points a game during his senior year.

Bob was best in track and field. As a sixteen-year-old he competed in the West Coast Relays and won the shot put, discus and high hurdles, tied for second in the high jump and ran the anchor leg on Tulare's winning relay team. This versatility gave Bob's coach, Virgil Jackson, an idea. He wrote to the Amateur Athletic Union for a book on the decathlon, the grueling competition that requires an amazing combination of skills. It consists of ten track and field events including dashes, hurdles, a distance race, jumps (high and broad), and the throwing events. Jackson hoped to prepare Bob to enter the decathlon in the 1952 Olympics, which were still four years away.

For several weeks Bob and his coach worked until darkness each evening. Then, merely to get a taste of competition, Bob entered the decathlon in a regional Olympic trial. To everyone's surprise, he won. Bob now decided to enter the 1948 Olympics. "But it's only six weeks away!" said Coach Jackson. Bob shrugged. He was determined to go to London to compete with the world's top athletes.

Although Bob was seasick during the transatlantic crossing, he seemed fully recovered when he arrived at Wembley Stadium in London on August 5th. Neither the 70,000 spectators nor the cold and rainy weather bothered him. In the first three events he did well. But in the high jump he ran into trouble. He missed his first two attempts at 5 feet, 9 inches, a height he had to clear if he hoped to remain in the running. On his third attempt, he cleared the bar and went on to win the event at six feet, 1¾ inches—the highest he had ever jumped. He did well in the next event, the 440-yard dash, too. After five events he was in third place, only 49 points behind the leader.

The next morning Bob was up at 7:00, ready for the final events. The rain was falling harder than it had the day before. First he ran the high hurdles and then he

Bob Mathias (right) skims over the hurdles in the 1948 Olympic decathlon competition.

went on to the discus throw—his best event. He threw it so far onto the grass that officials couldn't find the marker. They searched for more than an hour before giving him credit for a toss of 144 feet, 4 inches, less than he actually deserved.

In the eighth event, the pole vault, Bob won easily at 11 feet, 5½ inches. But now the pressure was really on him. Ignace Heinrich of France had already finished his ten events, scoring a total of 6,974 points. Bob's chance of winning now hinged on the javelin throw. It was 10:00 P.M., and the only light came from the flickering Olympic torch and a string of pale bulbs.

Bob lets the discus fly—on his way to an Olympic gold medal.

90

With his last bit of energy, Bob flung the spear 165 feet, 1 inch on his second try. He beat Heinrich's effort by 31 feet.

The big javelin victory was exactly what Mathias needed. All he had to do in the final event, the 1500-meter run, was jog around the track in six minutes or less. In the backstretch he seemed to stagger, but he sprinted the last 100 yards and crossed the finish line with 49 seconds to spare. His final point total jumped to 7,139. At the age of seventeen he had become the youngest track and field performer ever to win an Olympic gold medal, and he had done it in the most difficult event of all.

Bob returned home a hero. President Truman welcomed him back. Tulare temporarily renamed itself "Mathiasville." Two hundred girls proposed marriage by mail and phone. Companies offered him large sums of money for endorsements of their products. But Bob refused them all. He went to Kiski Prep School in Pennsylvania to improve his C-plus high-school average. While he was there, he did so well in football that he was swamped with offers from colleges all over the country. He finally chose Stanford, because it was close to home and because it offered him a fine education.

Bob's friends urged him to forget about football at Stanford; they were afraid he might be injured and ruin his chances for the 1952 Olympics. They seemed to be right: he was hurt three times during his first season. But each time Bob recovered, and he led Stanford to its first conference championship in twelve years. In his senior year, he gave up football to begin decathlon training again.

When Mathias arrived at Helsinki, Finland, for the 1952 Olympic Games, it was a case of the rest of the world against one man. As it turned out, the rest of the world didn't stand a chance. Despite a pulled thigh muscle, Bob practically clinched another gold medal on the first day of competition. He set a new world-record for total decathlon points.

Mathias never competed again, at least not in the decathlon. Instead, he turned to politics and in 1966 he was elected to the first of several terms as a member of the U.S. House of Representatives from California. He soon showed his versatility in politics, just as he had in sports where he twice proved he was the world's greatest athlete—not in one event, but in a combination of *ten*.

Mathias sails over the pole vault bar at 13 feet 8 inches.

Willie Mays

There were two outs in the ninth inning, and two strikes on Willie Mays. As Mays whipped his bat at the Houston pitcher's delivery, a Giant teammate on first base sped for second. Whup! Foul ball. Then another foul. Another. The Giants were two runs behind and Mays was deliberately spoiling pitch after pitch, waiting for the one he could lift into the stands for a game-tying homer. It was late in the 1965 season, and the Giants were still fighting for the pennant.

Whup! Six straight fouls. And then, with a crash, Mays connected. The ball zoomed over the center fielder's head and rocketed into the stands of the Houston Astrodome,

Willie follows through on a powerful swing.

450 feet from the plate.

"Fantastic!" said San Francisco catcher Tom Haller. "Everybody in the ball park knew he was going for a homer, and he got it." The Giants went on to win and another of Mays' jubilant teammates, Orlando Cepeda, exclaimed: "Willie Mays is amazing!"

But followers of Mays had long ago stopped being amazed by his deeds. They remembered, for example, a play that a younger Willie Mays had made eleven years earlier, in the opening game of the 1954 World Series. Batter Vic Wertz had swung hard and, at the crack of the bat, the 23-year-old Mays had turned his back to home plate and dashed toward the fence. He was still in full retreat from the diamond when he pulled down the tremendous drive. It was voted the sports thrill of the year. In later seasons, Mays made several outfield plays which he thought even better.

Running, fielding and batting, Willie Mays brought a special quality of excitement to the game. He would stroll languidly off base, then explode down the line so jet-fast he would run out from under his hat. Or he'd cup his hands for a waist-high "basket catch," turning a routine fly ball into an adventure. Or he would let his slim, 34-ounce bat drift lazily over the plate, then lash out and drive the pitch high and far into the stands. Even during a pre-game warmup in front of the dugout, Mays could give the spectators a show.

Walter Alston, manager of the Dodgers, once summed up the secret of Mays's attraction this way: "He plays the game as if it's fun." But no career can always be fun, even that of the irrepressible Willie Mays.

Running straight toward the outfield wall, Willie reaches up to nab Wertz's drive in the 1954 World Series.

As his years in baseball piled up and his role changed, the once playful star worked out his own definition of drudgery. "When I was a kid," he recalled, "it was all fun. Now there are times when it feels like work. But when it gets to be a job, that's when I'll quit." Still, Mays did not sound like a a man who would quit soon.

In the beginning, on the sandlots of Fairfield, Alabama, Mays played ball all the time. Willie's father taught his son to love the game he himself played—more for fun than profit—for a local semipro team.

"The biggest surprise of my life," says Willie, "was the day I found out folks paid

Leo Durocher, Willie's first big supporter in the majors, cheers him home after Willie's game winning home run in a 1954 game.

Dad money for playing baseball. That seemed to me just about the nicest idea that anyone ever thought up."

At sixteen, young Willie signed with the Birmingham Black Barons. At nineteen, his immense natural ability gained him a $6,000 bonus from the New York Giants and a position on their Class B farm team in Trenton, New Jersey. At twenty, he walloped top-grade minor league pitching for a .477 average in his first thirty-five games at Minneapolis, and was promoted directly to the Giants.

The major leagues were a new world for Mays, and it was anything but fun at first. He was so nervous that he went hitless in his first twenty-one times at bat. Manager Leo Durocher, who was to become a second father to the youngster, found him sobbing in front of his locker.

"Willie, don't worry," Durocher told him soothingly. "We're not sending you back to Minneapolis no matter what happens. Someday you'll laugh at all this."

Durocher was right. Soon Mays was so full of exuberance over his success in the big leagues that he would play a double-header at the Polo Grounds, then saunter into the streets of Harlem for a game of stickball with the kids.

In his rookie year, the Giants made a late-season rush to wrest the pennant from the Brooklyn Dodgers. That winter he was called into the Army. In 1954 he returned and won the Most Valuable Player Award, hitting 41 homers and leading the league with a batting average of .345.

In later years, personal problems plagued Mays—an unhappy marriage, a divorce, debts and near-bankruptcy. But none of the problems bothered him as much as the difficulties that followed the Giants' move to San Francisco in 1958. "I didn't have to get used to San Francisco," said Mays later.

94

Mays

"But it took San Francisco a while to accept me."

Mays bought a home in the St. Francis Woods section of San Francisco causing demonstrations of racial prejudice and anger. For a time, Mays and his son Michael moved back to the New York area. Some men might have fought back with understandable bitterness. But Mays saved his competitive spirit for the baseball field.

Fellow players marvel that Mays, whose strength is the envy of the league, does all his fighting within the framework of the game. He never brawls, never betrays a loss of temper. "I get mad," he once admitted. "But what good is it gonna do me to hit the wall and break my fingers? What good will that do the ball club? I get paid for playing ball."

Indeed, Mays became one of baseball's highest-paid performers at $125,000 a year. In 1964 he was named Giant captain, and was an advisor to many of the younger players. He was an All-Star Game regular. He clubbed 29 or more homers every year from 1954 through 1966, and always scored more than 100 runs.

In 1965 Mays was voted Most Valuable Player for the second time in his career. Then, during the 1966 season, he blasted his 535th homer to pass Jimmie Foxx in total home runs. Mays' total of 635 at the start of the 1972 season placed him second only to Babe Ruth, who hit 714.

Because Mays cannot make a half-effort, he occasionally dips too far into his reserve strength. After he collapsed on the field in 1962, manager Alvin Dark realized that he would have to rest Mays once in a while to prevent his playing himself right into the hospital.

Mays always plays hard. It distresses him sometimes that he gets tired in the heat of a pennant race. "I've got to concentrate so

Still a threat, veteran Mays waits for a pitch in 1971.

hard that I can't help out the other guys the way I should," he says unhappily. But his teammates think playing with Mays is more than enough—especially in the thick of a pennant battle. "It's wonderful seeing him all the time hustle, hustle," says former teammate Jesus Alou. "Willie taught me that's what baseball is all about."

Herman Franks, when he was managing the Giants, explained his field captain's value: "When we need a run," Franks said, "Mays gets it."

George Mikan

First there were titters, then guffaws. De-Paul University's gangling, 6-foot, 10-inch George Mikan stood blushing in the center of the basketball court at Madison Square Garden. Rhode Island State's coach, playing on the natural sympathy of the crowd for an underdog, had sent a 5-foot, 7-inch guard out to jump against Mikan at the start of the National Invitational Tournament semifinal.

The year was 1945. Any basketball player who stood more than 6-foot-6 was regarded in those days as a clumsy oaf better known for his altitude than his ability. George Mikan was no exception. Even his DePaul teammates sometimes jeered: "Mikan's girl is ten feet tall; she sleeps in the kitchen with her feet in the hall."

Jibes of that sort had long stung the unathletic-looking youth with thick glasses. But he had gradually learned that a crowd can be easily swayed. Before the Rhode Island State game was over that night, spectators in the country's most famous arena were on his side. Pivoting left and right, Mikan tirelessly snared rebounds and flicked deft passes to scurrying teammates as defenders converged on him two and three at a time. And he poured in a record of 53 points himself, as many as the whole Rhode Island team. Even in modern, pinball-scoring-style basketball, 53 points in a college game is a big achievement. In those days, it was almost unbelievable.

The New York crowd roared its acclaim. Mikan was assuredly the big man in De-Paul's 97–53 victory that night—and in the championship victory over Bowling Green the next night. But the fans could not know

that to Mikan his feat marked an even more important triumph: the victory over self-doubt.

The lanky lad from Joliet, Illinois, had been six feet tall at the age of eleven. For years he was so awkward, so self-conscious, that he finally tried to escape by enrolling in a Chicago seminary. A kindly priest told him, "The priesthood is no place for anybody who is trying to run away from something." He convinced Mikan to enroll at nearby DePaul University.

DePaul's coach, clever, energetic little Ray Meyer, cured George's self-consciousness and embarrassment. "He was a slave driver," said Mikan. "But he was just what I needed." The one-time tanglefoot was conscious of his own shortcomings and eager to improve. With Meyer, he worked long hours after teammates had finished practice. He skipped rope for twenty min-

DePaul coach Ray Meyer gives young Mikan some good advice.

96

utes a day; he shadow-boxed; he thumped a punching bag.

"I found that a tall man didn't have to accept clumsiness," Mikan said later. "He could be well-coordinated and graceful if he was willing to try hard enough to improve himself." Mikan was willing. He also struggled to curb his fiery temper. "Learn to be a good sport," Meyer told him. "You'll be surprised at what you can do."

The big fellow drilled and drilled on hook shots. As a DePaul sophomore, he learned to make them right-handed. As a junior, he developed the ability to bank in shots from both sides—shots that the tallest opponent found himself unable to block.

Mikan earned All-America recognition three years in succession. In the spring of 1946, he turned professional for a record annual salary of $12,000. Before his career ended, he doubled that income, made the pro all-star team six years in a row and led the Minneapolis Lakers to seven world titles in eight seasons. Broad-shouldered and bull-strong at 245 pounds, Mikan was voted basketball player of the half century in 1950 by the Associated Press.

Mikan revolutionized the professional game and became its number-one gate attraction at a time when poor attendance might have set back the sport for decades. Pro basketball's early years were difficult.

The teams traveled to small cities by car and train. They played in drafty armories and auditoriums. It was especially hard for an extra-large center who had to sleep diagonally across two regular hotel beds in order to get a good night's sleep. And to Mikan, sleep was perhaps the most important part of conditioning. He insisted on getting twelve hours of sleep a night. Mikan collected an assortment of bruises and welts from overeager foes and lost 30 to 35 pounds a season. But despite his difficulties

Mikan goes up for a shot while his opponents are helpless to block it.

he missed only two games in eight seasons.

Crowds would boo the Lakers' brawny No. 99 when he whirled out of a pivot, elbows flying. ("When they play rough, I play rough," he reasoned.) But they flocked to see him perform. Night after night, he dumped 28, 29, 30 points into the basket. "Everyone forgets," observed rival coach Joe Lapchick, "that Mikan is also the best feeder from the pivot this game ever had.

97

Cover him normally and he kills you with his scoring. Cover him abnormally and he murders you with passes."

So masterful was Mikan's work under the basket that in 1951 the National Basketball Association widened the foul lane—where players with the ball were limited to a stay of three seconds—from six to ten feet. "The wider lane makes it tougher for me," Mikan conceded, "but it makes the game better than it ever was before." The following year, he set a personal scoring mark with a 61-point splurge.

Mikan wanted to succeed off the court, too. He tried to study law while traveling from town to town in the NBA, but three times he failed his bar exam. At the age of thirty he determined to quit playing and concentrate on his future as a lawyer. He got his law degree but his break with basketball didn't last very long.

A few months after his 1954 retirement, Mikan became general manager of the Minneapolis Lakers. Two years later he returned to the league as a player, a decision prompted by more than 1,500 letters from fans of the Minneapolis–St. Paul area. "Since I had asked the people of this area to back the Lakers, they insisted that I practice what I preached," he explained with a laugh.

In 1957, Mikan even took over the coaching job for thirty-nine games. Then he left basketball for a brief whirl at politics and, finally, a highly paid job as Minneapolis representative of a Wall Street brokerage firm. Mikan's ability to deal well with people in business came as no surprise. He had already proved that he usually succeeded in what he set out to do.

The Lakers' star center hooks in a shot against the College All-Stars.

Bus Mosbacher

Many times he had heard the sound of a cannon—in World War II as a naval officer and in peacetime as a skipper of racing sailboats. But for Emil "Bus" Mosbacher, Jr., no cannon roared as magnificently as the one that gave the traditional salute when he crossed the finish line for the 1962 America's Cup competition.

It was a September afternoon on the Atlantic Ocean off Newport, Rhode Island. Mosbacher had steered *Weatherly,* a 68-foot sailboat representing the United States, across the finish line ahead of Australia's *Gretel* and had successfully defended yachting's most valued trophy, the America's Cup, the prize in sailing's World Series.

The Cup dates back to 1851, when the schooner *America* first won the trophy from an English schooner in a race around England's Isle of Wight. Since then millions of dollars have been spent by challenging nations in unsuccessful efforts to win it back from the United States. Millions more have been spent by the New York Yacht Club in defense of the "ould mug," which originally cost only 100 guineas (about $500) and doesn't even have a bottom on it.

Although the money for designing, building and campaigning the boats has always been an enormous factor in America's Cup rivalry, in the end it is the men who sail the ships—the skippers and their crews—who make the difference. Bus Mosbacher made that difference in 1962 when, at age forty, he capped a lifetime of sailing achievements by winning the Cup.

As a boy in White Plains, New York,

Weatherly *and* Gretel *cross the starting line in the deciding race of the 1962 America's Cup.*

99

near Long Island Sound, Bus was fortunate in having a father who liked sailing and could afford it. "Dad put me in my first boat when I was five," recalled Bus, whose nickname is the shortened form of Buster.

To play baseball, football, tennis and basketball, all one needs is a ball, and a glove, a racquet or a bat. In sailing, one cannot simply be given a boat and launched onto the ocean. Sailing is a science that requires preparation and study (of wind, sails, maneuvers and the parts of a boat), stamina, agility and determination, and an instinctive feel for the wheel or the tiller.

Some people are content after they've learned sailing fundamentals to be cruising sailors. They sail at a leisurely pace, without the need for competition. Others, like Bus Mosbacher, must be in the race.

As young Bus was to discover, racing sailboats come in many sizes. They range from single-sail catboats, less than ten feet long, to America's Cup craft, measuring roughly 68 feet (referred to as 12-meter boats), to ocean racers, exceeding 70 feet and carrying several sails. Bus was to learn that boats of the same design (Snipes, Stars, Blue Jays, Finns and so on) race within their own class, with unlimited numbers of boats in the race. In current America's Cup racing, however, just two similar boats, conforming to what is known as the 12-meter formula, race against one another in what is called a match-race.

By the time Bus was ten years old, he was a full-fledged skipper of a 22-foot, 10-inch Star-class boat. Four years later he was sailing a 30½-foot Atlantic-class boat and his younger brother, Bob, was given the Star. "As soon as we did well in one class, Dad would move us up to a tougher one," Bus said.

It was not enough for Mosbacher to be outstanding among other young sailors,

winning Long Island Sound midget and junior titles. While barely in his teens, he was also tossed into competition with sailors who had been racing for decades. Frequently he beat them, demonstrating the

A true skipper with an eye to the wind and a hand to the wheel.

agility of mind and body necessary to a great champion, on land or sea.

Bus attended Choate School and Dartmouth College, and continued to collect racing trophies. These awards encompassed many racing classes on many fronts—from frostbite (winter) competition and 33½-foot International one-design races to ocean-racing contests on Long Island Sound, in southern waters and off the English Coast.

Bus had received world recognition as a superb skipper long before he accepted an invitation to take the wheel of an America's Cup contender, *Vim,* in 1958. In that year, after a 21-year lapse, competition for the treasured trophy was resumed between the United States and England.

His crews already knew that Bus didn't lose his temper when something went wrong in a race. Calm and collected, he could remain silent, yet convey all he wanted to say. As Bus himself admitted, "My crew knows something is wrong when they see tears coming down my cheeks."

But beneath his gentle, courteous facade is a man who considers sailboat racing as "combat" and who is a brilliant and decisive skipper of any boat he commands.

Larry Marx, who has sailed with Bus since they were boys, said of him: "He has an ability to concentrate for longer periods of time than anyone I know. He is always thinking and working, looking for that little something—that little puff of wind, that sudden tactical mistake by an opponent—that will enable his boat to move faster than anyone else's."

In assuming the helm of *Vim* in 1958, Bus took charge of a boat that was more than twenty years old and in competition with three new United States boats, *Columbia, Weatherly* and *Easterner.* He was hoping to defeat the other boats in the trials

so that he could compete against England's *Sceptre* in the Cup race. Defeating the new boats was considered impossible, but Bus and his crew almost did it. They beat *Weatherly* and *Easterner,* only to lose by a close margin to *Columbia.*

The Cup is awarded to the boat that wins four races against its opponent in a best-of-seven series. *Columbia* went on to sweep England's *Sceptre* in the first four races.

In 1962 Bus decided to try again, this time at the helm of *Weatherly,* in the trials. His competition included *Columbia* and *Nefertiti,* a new craft. He gathered a devoted, able crew of ten, many of whom had crewed on *Vim* four years earlier. Each was an expert at his assignment.

As skipper, Mosbacher was the quarterback, coach and manager, the one who had to make the hundreds of split-second decisions. He and his aides spent many months of preparation before the actual trials. Then they practiced long and hard on the starts for which Bus was famous and on the precision sail-handling that would promise precious seconds in a race. Mosbacher's skillful starts in the 1958 trial races had already stamped him as a master of this important phase of the sport. In match-racing the race is frequently won at the beginning even though the races are held over courses of more than twenty miles. Before the starting gun, each skipper tries to get his boat into a favorable position so that when the starting gun goes off he can interfere with the wind of the other boat and have his own wind clear.

Bus's wizardry on these starts enabled *Weatherly* to prevail in the 1962 trials. Then came the actual Cup races against *Gretel.* The Australian entry managed to win only one race. Bus and *Weatherly* kept the Cup by a 4–1 margin.

In 1967, Bus took the helm of a new 12-

meter sloop, *Intrepid*. Once again he sailed a victorious course for America, this time defeating Australia's *Dame Pattie* in four straight races.

The measure of a great athlete varies with the sport. An America's Cup skipper needs more mind than muscle. He needs discipline in the direction of both himself and his crew; he needs the ability to make a lifetime of sailing experience pay off in a single critical decision. He needs courage and conviction. Bus Mosbacher has all these qualities.

President Nixon recognized the value of this commanding nature and on January 12, 1967 appointed Mosbacher his Chief of Protocol. The nation's premier helmsman became responsible for planning the visits of dignitaries, and shepherding them through the maze of official Washington.

Captain Mosbacher races off Newport, Rhode Island.

Stan Musial

The batboy was coming in to pitch. His team of tough, strong men from the local zinc mill was playing poorly. The team had fallen far behind early in the game and victory seemed impossible. The manager decided he had nothing to lose. "Get in there," he told the batboy. "Let's see what you can do."

For a long time the manager had been teaching the batboy, Stan Musial, how to throw fastballs, curveballs and change-ups. Now, he wanted to see the fifteen-year-old in action. He thought the boy would do all right. The players thought the manager was playing a joke.

Stan walked to the mound. He was tall and lean—and nervous. What boy wouldn't be nervous coming in to play against grown men?

Stan began whipping in pitches. He fired hard with a flapping left-handed motion and he struck out a batter. Soon he struck out another. And another. Now nobody thought it was a joke. The boy continued throwing hard and he kept on striking out men. In six innings he struck out thirteen players.

The sports fans in Donora, Pennsylvania, suddenly realized they had a very special young athlete in their town. They watched with interest and rooted hard as Stan began playing basketball and baseball for the local high school. In 1938, shooting smooth, accurate, left-handed hook shots, he led the

Eighteen year old Stan Musial, a pitcher at Williamson, West Virginia, poses in the uncut grass of the home-town field.

Donora High basketball team through an undefeated season. For three seasons he was the best hitter and pitcher on the Donora High baseball team.

Stan graduated from high school in June, 1938. He was now seventeen years old, and it was time for him to think about a career. His father, Lukasz Musial, had come to the United States from Poland. He had little education and had worked very hard for little money all his life.

He wanted Stan to go to college so he could have a better life. But Stan preferred to sign a professional baseball contract.

Stan demonstrates his awkward batting stance.

After many long arguments, Stan's mother said, "This is a free country, Lukasz. The boy is free not to go to college." Lukasz finally decided she was right.

Stan signed a contract with the St. Louis Cardinals and began pitching for their Class D minor league team at Williamson, West Virginia. In two seasons at Williamson, he won fifteen games and lost eight. He was earning only $70 a month, but it was enough to keep him stuffed with hamburgers and frankfurters and he was doing what he wanted to do most in life. He was happy.

In 1940 Stan was playing for Daytona Beach, Florida, in a higher minor league. On August 11, a day he was not scheduled to pitch, he was sent out to play center field. During the game he raced in for a low line drive, tumbled, caught the ball and fell heavily on his left shoulder. He didn't know how seriously he had injured his shoulder until he tried to pitch again. Then he suddenly discovered that there was no longer any snap in his pitches. His arm was dead. As the season rolled on, he realized that he would never again be a good pitcher.

Stan visited his manager, Dickie Kerr, and sadly said he was quitting baseball. "You can't quit," Dickie said. "You've got a future, Stan. You can hit. The Cardinals will keep you as an outfielder."

Stan decided to give it a try. The next season, 1941, he was given a chance with Springfield in the Western Association. His arm was not as strong as it once had been, but it was strong enough for outfield throwing. He played well in the outfield for Springfield and he hit very well. He would stand at the plate in the strangely coiled left-handed stance that would one day become the most famous in baseball. His legs were close together, his body was twisted and his head would peek out from behind his hunched right shoulder. He would un-

104

The National League All-Stars crowd around to congratulate Stan after he has hit the game-winning 12th inning home run in the 1955 All-Star game.

coil and swing as the pitch came in and he would wallop long line drives.

He batted .379 and hit 26 home runs at Springfield, and was promoted at mid-season to Rochester of the International League, just a step away from the majors. He batted .326 in 54 games at Rochester and was called up to the Cardinals at the end of the season. There he batted .426 in 12 games.

"Stan the Man," as he was frequently called, played with the St. Louis Cardinals from September, 1941, until September 29, 1963. He became the greatest National League hitter of his time, one of the best of all time. He batted higher than .340 in seven separate seasons. He won seven National League batting championships and two runs-batted-in championships. He was the league's Most Valuable Player three times and he led the Cardinals to four pen-

nants and three world championships.

Musial had many great moments. He once walloped five home runs against the Giants in one double-header. He hit a twelfth-inning home run to win the 1955 All-Star Game, and he made nine hits in 11 at-bats in a two-day 1948 series against the Dodgers. He batted .330 in 1962, when he was forty-two years old—old enough by pro baseball standards to be "over the hill." He played in 895 consecutive games from 1952 through 1957, setting a National League record.

Stan made 3,630 hits in his career, the second highest total in major league history. He had 725 doubles, 177 triples, 475 homers, 1,951 runs batted in and a .331 lifetime batting average.

Although he was one of the great players of his time, Stan never became over-whelmed by his own importance. "Some

Musial scores, seeming to smile as he avoids the tag of Reds catcher Ed Bailey. The umpire seems less pleased.

players can remember exactly what they hit in a certain game," he once said. "I'm not too good at that. I just enjoy playing ball. Sure, I like my hits as much as the next guy does, and I'd be kidding if I said I didn't get pleasure out of my records. But in a ball game I'm mostly interested in winning."

He was also interested in people. He was friendly with rookies, writers and fans. He appreciated the attention others paid to him. And no matter how large the crowd of autograph-seekers, no matter how many intrusions people made on his private life, he was always polite, always obliging. "It

is difficult to write about Stan Musial," Ed Linn once noted, "without sounding as if you were delivering the nominating address at a Presidential convention."

When Stan retired in 1963 he was a popular and wealthy man. He was offered many jobs and he accepted one as vice-president of the Cardinals. Later, he accepted another offer, becoming head of the President's Council on Youth Fitness.

But he couldn't resist the lure of full-time baseball. And in 1967 Stan the Man returned —not as a player, of course, but in the vital role of general manager of his only team, the Cardinals.

106

Bronko Nagurski

He weighed about 230 pounds when he played football and he was six-feet, one-inch tall, but to hear people talk you'd think he weighed 400 pounds and stood ten feet tall. In fact, Bronko Nagurski did so many unbelievable things in football that it is already hard to distinguish fact from fancy. He has become a legend.

Bronko grew up in the lake country of Minnesota, the wild, rough land near the Canadian border. Although he played football in high school, college scouts didn't pay much attention to the teams in his part of Minnesota. So when he arrived at the University of Minnesota in September, 1926, none of the coaches had ever heard of him.

Nagurski rented a room near the campus, registered for classes and reported for freshman football tryouts. He was 18 years old and he idolized the varsity stars. As he stood in line during the first workout, awaiting his turn to hit the tackling dummy, he glanced across the field to where the varsity was practicing. Soon he was staring spellbound at the varsity and he didn't realize it was his turn to hit the dummy.

"Hit that dummy!" the freshman coach yelled.

Nagurski snapped around, charged and hit it.

"Hit it again!" the coach yelled.

The freshman hit it again, knocking it from its moorings.

"What's your name?" the coach asked.

"Bronko Nagurski," the freshman answered.

The name meant nothing to the coach, but that didn't matter. What mattered was that this big fellow could hit as hard as anyone the coach had ever seen. Within minutes he had taken Bronko to meet Doc Spears, the varsity coach.

"Where are you from, boy?" Spears asked.

Bronko said he was from International Falls, Minnesota, and that he had played high school football at Bemidji, Minnesota.

"What position did you play?"

"Fullback," said Bronko. "And guard and tackle and wherever else they needed me."

Spears told Bronko to hit the tackling dummy, and Bronko hit it. Spears smiled and nodded. He patted Bronko on the back and said, simply: "Get plenty of sleep."

Bronko got plenty of sleep and he played plenty of football for the freshman team. And the following year he began playing tackle for Spears' varsity. On defense Bronko would dig in, charge and knock down blockers until he could grab the ball-carrier. On offense he would bang down opponents and open big holes for the Minnesota backs.

Minnesota's most important game in 1927 was against Notre Dame. As usually happened in those days, Notre Dame, coached by Knute Rockne, was a heavy favorite. Notre Dame went ahead, 7–0, and held the lead into the fourth quarter. With the game coming to a close, Notre Dame lined up to punt. As the punter grabbed the ball, Bronko charged. As the punter kicked, Bronko leaped. Suddenly, the ball was on the ground, buried under a pile of players. The players rose, one by one, until only one man was on the ground. He was Bronko and he had the ball in his hands.

Minnesota ran four running plays. On each, Herb Joesting, the fullback, carried the ball and Bronko led the interference. On the fourth play, Joesting followed Bronko into the end zone. Minnesota tied Notre Dame that day, 7–7.

Minnesota went on to bigger glory the next season, 1928, when Bronko began playing fullback. Against Iowa early in the season, Bronko knocked down a defensive back and ran right over him to score a touchdown. Bronko broke three ribs on the play and could not play fullback against Northwestern the next week. But he did play tackle. And he was as spectacular as ever.

Late in November, Minnesota and unbeaten Wisconsin were tied, 0–0, in the fourth quarter. A Wisconsin back carried the ball to his own 20-yard line, where he was hit hard by Bronko. The ball flew into the air, Bronko grabbed it and sped toward the goal line. He was hit once, hit again, hit a third time. Each time he kept going, dragging the Wisconsin players into the end zone with him. Years later someone told Bronko what a thrill it had been watching him drag five tacklers over the goal line. "Six," Bronko said quietly. "There were six."

In 1929 Bronko was again a versatile star. Grantland Rice wrote, "Bronko Nagurski is the only man who ever lived who could lead his own interference." After the season, one newspaper named only ten men to fill the eleven positions on its All-America team. One of the men, Bronko Nagurski, filled two positions: tackle and fullback.

Bronko joined the Chicago Bears the next season to play pro football. In his first game against the Green Bay Packers, he was the deep blocker whenever Chicago punted. Green Bay's Cal Hubbard, the biggest and best tackle in pro football, called aside Bronko's teammate, Red Grange, and said, "Next time you punt, let me by. I won't block it. I just want to get a shot at Nagurski. I've been hearing about how hard

Bronko (holding the ball) is brought down in the end zone.

he is and I want a crack at him."

Grange, also eager to find out how tough the rookie was, let Hubbard through. Nagurski smashed Hubbard straight back. "That's enough," Hubbard told Grange. "Now I know."

Nagurski played fullback on offense and tackle on defense for the Bears. He starred at both positions. He was a crunching blocker and a tough tackler. He even passed on occasion. But he is remembered most as a thundering runner. "Defense him?" New York Giant coach Steve Owen once said. "There's only one defense that could stop Nagurski—shoot him before he leaves the dressing room."

Bronko played with the Bears for seven years, retiring after the 1937 season. He spent some time as a professional wrestler, then returned to Minnesota. He fished and hunted in the lake country and farmed his 120 acres of land. But he was to have one more try in the professional leagues.

In 1943 the nation was at war and many athletes were in service. The Bears needed players and they asked Bronko to give them one more season. Although he hadn't played football in six years, he agreed. He played most of the season at tackle. The Bears' final game was with the Chicago Cardinals (now in St. Louis) and they needed to win to become conference champions. Coach Hunk Anderson asked Bronko if he would play "a little fullback," and Bronko agreed.

In the fourth quarter, with the Cardinals ahead, 24–14, Anderson put Bronko in the backfield. Time after time, Bronko crashed through the Cardinal line. He was 35, but he was running just as he had when he was 25. He brought the ball to the goal line. Then he smashed over. The Bears kicked the extra point and trailed, 24–21.

The Cardinals couldn't move the ball,

The Bronk gallops for a big gain in the 1937 title game against Washington.

and the Bears took over again. They drove down the field but were stopped at the Cardinal 33-yard line. It was fourth down with four yards to go for a first down. There were four minutes left in the game. If the Bears failed to make the first down, they would lose the ball. They might never get it back.

They called upon Bronko. He clutched the ball, lowered his head and rammed straight ahead. The Bears needed four yards. Bronko got them six. Seconds later the Bears scored the game-winning touchdown.

After that last great performance, Bronko retired for good. But he had already become a football legend.

109

Joe Namath

On January 9, 1969, at a football banquet at the Miami Springs Villa, Joe Namath was receiving an award as the outstanding player of 1968. He approached the microphone on the dais to deliver, presumably, a brief acceptance speech. But Namath used the opportunity instead to make a daring prediction. He told the audience, "We will win on Sunday . . . I guarantee you."

The prediction was daring because Namath's team, the Jets, were 18-point underdogs to Baltimore. Yet three days later in the Orange Bowl before a crowd of 75,-000 and a national television audience of about 60 million, the Jets fulfilled Namath's prophecy. Joe led his team up and down the field with the confidence of a conquering general. After 60 minutes, the Jets had accomplished what seemed impossible—they defeated the Colts, 16–7.

Namath was superb. His statistics for the day: 17 passes completed in 28 attempts, no interceptions, and 206 yards gained. As he left the field, the index finger of his right hand pointed toward the sky, proclaiming that the Jets were No. 1.

Joe Namath became more than a football star—he became a sort of folk hero as well. Unlike the serious, clean-cut stars of the past, Joe Willie seemed mischievous, a kind

Joe Namath calls signals during the 1969 Super Bowl game.

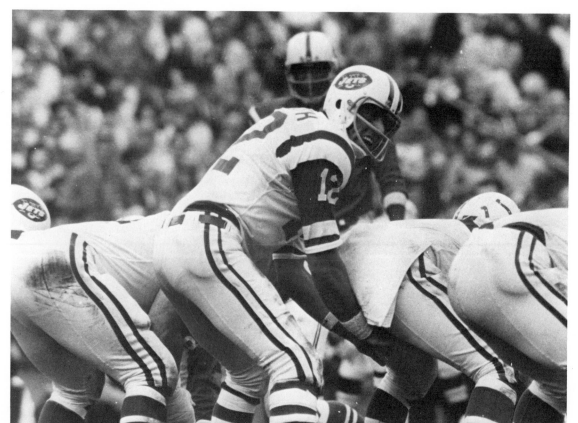

Joe gets off a pass for Alabama against Texas in the Orange Bowl.

of "bad boy." Magazines and newspapers immediately carried long stories about him. Book publishers rushed biographies of him into print. Television networks and giant corporations invited him to make personal appearances. Although traditional fans considered him bad for sports, it seemed that everyone else wanted to know more about "Broadway Joe."

Life did not begin glamorously for Joseph Alexander Namath. He was born in Beaver Falls, Pennsylvania on Memorial Day, 1943. The air in Beaver Falls was often thick with the gray smoke belched from nearby steel plants. Joe was the fourth son of Rose and John Namath. His father earned his living making steel tubes for boilers.

"Joey started throwing a football when he was big enough to walk," his mother remembered. "His brothers, Bobby and Franklin, always got up football games in the front yard. Joey was just five and too little to play, but the boys needed a quarterback. So Joey was it. When the games started, he had to throw the ball or get knocked down by his brothers. They didn't take pity on Joey at all."

The front-lawn lessons apparently stayed with Joe Namath for some time. He always preferred playing quarterback to any other position. When he was 10 years old he played in the Pop Warner League. From there, it was junior high and high school football. As a senior he led Beaver Falls High to an undefeated season and its first league championship in 32 years.

Already a budding star, Joe went to the University of Alabama, a football powerhouse. He soon became Alabama's starting quarterback, but he also developed a problem that would plague him throughout his career. In the fourth game of his senior season, against North Carolina State, he went on a roll-out to his right. When he attempted to cut back to his left, his knee collapsed. Then, just before his final game for Alabama—the Orange Bowl against Texas—the knee collapsed again on a routine play during a workout.

Another quarterback started for Alabama. But Namath was summoned off the bench when Alabama fell behind, 14–0. Despite his injury, he put on one of his most illustrious performances. He threw for two touchdowns, completed 18 of 37 passes for 255 yards and was voted the game's Most Valuable Player. But Alabama lost, 21–17.

The St. Louis Cardinals wanted to pick Namath first in the National Football League draft. But the New York Jets of the young American Football League were interested too. They offered Joe $400,000 to join them and he signed.

The American League did not have the established stars of the NFL and Namath immediately became the most expensive and most publicized player in the AFL. He quickly captured public interest and helped the upstart league toward mass acceptance. At the same time as the Jets were inching along the path to respectability, Namath was maturing as a pro quarterback.

111

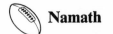

In 1966 and 1967, he led the AFL in completions and yards gained passing. But it wasn't until 1968 that the Jets started winning consistently. That season they won the Eastern Conference title in the AFL and defeated the Oakland Raiders, 27–23, for the league championship. The victory also earned them a place in Super Bowl III against the Baltimore Colts.

The National League Green Bay Packers had easily won the first two Super Bowl games against the Kansas City Chiefs and the Oakland Raiders. The Chiefs and Raiders had gone out of their way to publicly praise the Packers.

But going into the third Super Bowl Namath apparently decided that it was time the AFL stopped taking the gentlemanly approach. He started a week of psychological warfare by declaring that Earl Morrall, the quarterback for the Colts, was not as good as at least five quarterbacks in the AFL. Joe followed up with two other impertinent acts: he argued with Lou Michaels, a Colt player, in front of newsmen in a Miami restaurant. "I'll pick you apart," Joe boasted. Finally, he predicted a Jet victory. The rest of the Jets rallied around Namath.

The Jets led, 7–0 at halftime and 13–0 after three periods. It was 16–0 in the fourth quarter when Baltimore put its only score on the board. Although Jim Turner, the kicker, accounted for 10 of the Jets' points (three field goals and an extra point) and Matt Snell, the running back, scored the only touchdown, it was Joe Namath who emerged from the game larger than life.

The Jets' win was also a big boost for the AFL. After eight years of fighting for acceptance they had finally shown that they could equal the NFL. Shortly afterward the leagues completed a merger in which the AFL took a full and equal part.

Namath, meanwhile, branched out from his role as the dragon-slaying quarterback. He spent time as the host of television talk shows and he made several movies. In 1970

Namath looks downfield for his receivers.

112

he threatened to retire from pro football after being ordered by the league to sell a bar he owned. He returned, but soon broke a bone in his throwing hand and sat out most of the season. The Jets had to settle for second place instead of first.

Namath approached the 1971 season with renewed vigor. He hoped to prove that he was still the best quarterback in the game. In August, in the Jets' first pre-season game against the Detroit Lions, Namath tried to tackle a Lion who was running with a re-covered fumble. Since it was merely an exhibition game, Joe could have allowed the runner to score unscathed. But he went after him. After the whistle blew, Namath remained on the ground, clutching his good knee. It had been ripped apart and surgery was required immediately. He was sidelined for most of the 1971 season.

After the game, Namath was asked why he risked injury—and his future—by tack-ling a man he didn't have to pursue. "I only know how to play football one way," he answered.

By the end of November, Namath was back in uniform. The Jets had already been eliminated from the title race. But they were playing San Francisco, which was battling for the championship in its division. Bob Davis, Namath's replacement, was injured. Joe had to go into the game with the Jets trailing, 24–0. The 64,000 fans at Shea Stadium stood up and cheered as Joe made his first regular appearance of the season.

Namath played spectacularly. He com-pleted 11 out of 27 passes for 258 yards and three touchdowns. As the final seconds ticked away, Joe moved the Jets into scoring territory again. But two incomplete passes and then a 49er interception ended the threat. The Jets lost, 24–21.

Despite controversies and losses, Namath had already proved himself one of the great quarterbacks. When he played, he only knew how to play one way.

Coming back after his injury in 1971, Joe listens to Jet coach Weeb Ewbank.

Jack Nicklaus

From the moment Jack Nicklaus burst on the professional golf scene in 1962, there was no doubt that he would become a winner. He had dominated amateur golf for the previous few seasons while still a student at Ohio State University, in his hometown of Columbus, Ohio. He had won two U. S. Amateur Championships before his twenty-first birthday, and had played remarkably well in his few encounters with professionals. Already he had acquired such nicknames as "The Golden Bear" and "Baby Beef" because of his burly, 200-pound frame and his ability to hit brutally long shots.

Golf has always had at least one long-hitting star. No long hitter, however, can match Nicklaus for both distance and accuracy. His massive build plus his unique whiplash wrists produced a true phenomenon. Nicklaus has virtually demolished courses that for years had held a reputation for toughness.

In the 1960 World Amateur Championship at Merion, Pennsylvania, Nicklaus astonished golf fans everywhere when he shot 269—11 under par. Until then the best 72-hole score ever posted on the famous old Merion was Ben Hogan's 287 in the 1950 U. S. Open. In 1961 Jack won his second U. S. Amateur Championship at Pebble Beach, California, on one of the severest golf courses in the country. He captured his six matches in a total of 28-under par.

Still, Nicklaus had not proved he could stand the weekly grind of a touring pro. But in 1962, his first year as a professional, he disproved the story that he was nothing but a boy wonder who had not really felt the pressure of playing for big money. Jack won a check in every one of the 26 tournaments in which he competed. He finished among the top ten in sixteen of these tournaments and won more official money ($61,868.95) than any first-year player in golf history. He placed third on the prize list and, perhaps most amazing, he became the youngest golfer, at twenty-one, to win the U. S. Open Championship in forty years. The Open was played at Oakmont Country Club near Pittsburgh, not far from Arnold Palmer's hometown. Nicklaus defeated Palmer in an 18-hole play-off before a wildly partisan Palmer crowd.

Jack completed this sensational year by defeating Arnold Palmer and Gary Player

This is how Jack Nicklaus would look if a golf ball could see.

114

in the so-called "World Series of Golf," a television spectacular played at the Firestone Country Club in Akron, Ohio. He won the $50,000 first prize and boosted his earnings for the year to more than $110,000. In one year he had become one of modern golf's Big Three: Palmer, Player and Nicklaus. Since then, he has only enhanced his position among the game's modern greats.

In 1963, his second year on the tour, Jack won the Masters Championship and the National PGA, two of the four big titles in golf. In 1964 he didn't win one of the big titles, but he placed so consistently near the top that he edged out Palmer for the leading money winner's title, taking $113,-284 to Palmer's $113,203. Then, in 1965, he really exploded.

Just as he had done at Pebble Beach, Merion and Oakmont, Nicklaus ripped apart the Augusta National course in the Masters tournament and posted a winning score of 271, 17 under par. The course record of 274 had been set in 1953 and had seemed incredible, but now Nicklaus had bettered it by three shots. In golf, this

Nicklaus blasts out of a sand trap during the televised World Series of Golf in 1963.

was the equivalent of running the 100-yard dash in 9 seconds or hitting 65 home runs.

"The Golden Bear" has finished among the top four money winners every year. In 1971 he became the first man to win more than $200,000 in a single season on the PGA tour when he won a record $244,-490.50. His career earnings exceeded $1,-383,000, second on the all-time list.

Jack Nicklaus was the son of a fairly well-to-do owner of a chain of drugstores in Columbus, Ohio. His father constantly encouraged him to pursue sports, and frequently goaded the boy on by betting that he couldn't win in some sports event or other. "He once said I was too chubby to run track in junior high," Jack recalls. "So I went out and won three races."

In high school, Nicklaus also excelled in baseball and basketball. He was so well coordinated that he had a 90 percent average on foul shots, and averaged 18 points per game as a backcourt player.

But he always leaned toward golf. Receiving his first set of clubs at the age of 10, he immediately went out to Scioto Country Club, where the family were members, and shot a 51 on nine holes. He then began taking lessons from head pro Jack Grout, and by the time he was 16, he was Ohio Open champion.

Nicklaus has no secrets to account for his amazing ability. "Playing all the other sports apparently helped my coordination, and I've applied it to golf," he said. "I have fairly strong legs and hands, and I've worked hard to get them into my swing. Practice and hard work is the answer. My folks still like to chide me that I can't beat this fellow, or that one, or can't win a certain tournament. It makes me try harder, I suppose."

Jack is a steady, unemotional player. He sometimes seems almost bored when he's in

Jack gives his putt some encouragement during the last round of the 1966 Masters. The putt went in and Jack went on to win in a play-off.

the midst of winning a tournament. He is almost never discouraged by a poor shot, or a bad round. It only drives him more quickly to the practice tee. Since he displays few emotions, crowds have been unable to warm up to him, except when he comes down the stretch to win another tournament. He is a conservative dresser, and plays slowly. He smiles often and gently tips his cap to applause, but he has yet to gain the popularity enjoyed by other top players, such as Arnold Palmer or Gary Player.

In time, Nicklaus may finally win the popularity that others have received so easily as well as the top prizes. If he continues to improve, new golf courses may even have to be built to keep "Baby Beef" interested in the game.

116

Jesse Owens

At the age of six, James Cleveland Owens had been picking cotton in an Alabama field. But his family, like so many other Southern Negro families had spent enough of their lives as sharecroppers and had moved to the north. The Owens family moved to Cleveland, Ohio. When James Cleveland attended his first day of classes in his new grammar school, his teacher asked him his name.

"J. C., ma'am," he answered, because that was what his family called him.

"Jesse?" she said, confused by his drawl.

"Yes, ma'am," he said, eager to agree with anything his new teacher said. And so he began his new life with a new name, a name that someday would be known the world over: Jesse Owens.

Jesse first showed his great running ability when he was a teenager. At a high-school track meet, he crouched down in the starting blocks, burst forward and ran a 100-yard dash in 9.4 seconds, setting a national scholastic record that would stand for thirty years. Soon he was setting records not only in 100-yard dashes, but also in 200-yard dashes and in the broad jump. And he was doing it on an empty stomach.

Food was scarce in Jesse's home all the time he was in high school. His father had been injured in an auto accident and was not able to work. The family just managed to get along.

Jesse's life was still difficult when he became a student at Ohio State University. Though he had been a prominent high-school track star, he did not receive an athletic scholarship. He operated an office building elevator from 5:00 P.M. until 12:30 A.M. for $150 a month. After work

117

he traveled home by trolley car, ate dinner and slept until 6:30 A.M. He attended classes from eight in the morning to three in the afternoon, then practiced with the track squad until it was time to tend his elevator. He studied during the weekends and at spare moments in the elevator.

Despite the stiff schedule, he did well in his classes and in athletics. In 1933 he broke the world indoor broad-jump record,

Jesse Owens wins the broad jump in a 1935 N.C.A.A. meet in Berkeley, California.

then began starring in outdoor competition. About a week before the Big Ten outdoor meet, he pulled back the covers of his bed and discovered a dead snake on the sheets. He found out who had played the joke on him, and tracked the fellow down with a bag of water. He hit the jokester over the head with it, then turned to run away. He slipped and tumbled down a flight of stairs.

Jesse wrenched his back in the tumble and was in pain all week long. The day of the Big Ten meet he drove to the University of Michigan stadium with pain shooting through his back, thighs and knees. At the stadium he dispensed with his warm up to conserve his energy for the actual competition. When broad jumpers were called to the pit, he walked there slowly. Then with pain still shooting through his body, he raced down the approach strip and leaped into the air. He leaped 26 feet, 8¼ inches, a world record.

Then he ran the 100-yard dash in 9.4 seconds, tying the world record. After that he ran the 200-yard dash in a record 20.3 seconds and the 220-yard low hurdles in a record 22.6 seconds. Despite his agony, he had won four events, set three world records and tied one.

Jesse continued to amaze people. He went to the Olympic Games in 1936 and was confronted with as much pressure as any athlete has ever faced. The Games were held in Berlin, Germany, where Adolf Hitler had recently come to power. Throughout the Olympics, Nazi storm troopers paraded around Berlin shouting, "Heil Hitler." Hitler had repeatedly told the Germans that they were the greatest people on earth and that Jews and Negroes were inferior peoples. Some months earlier Germany's heavyweight boxer, Max Schmeling, had defeated America's Negro heavyweight, Joe Louis (a defeat that would be avenged).

Now, Hitler's followers said, Germany's track-and-field athletes would defeat more American champions.

In the finals of the 100-meter-dash competition, Jesse snapped forward as the starter's gun barked and began running on the soggy track. Head high, body straight, fists slightly clenched, he pulled away at the halfway mark and won the race by three feet. His time was 10.3 seconds, tying the world record. Hitler, who had personally congratulated nearly every other gold medalist, walked out of the stadium.

Then came the broad-jump trials. To qualify for the finals, Jesse had to leap only 23 feet, 5½ inches. He had surpassed that distance countless times, but this time he was having trouble. He was allowed three tries to leap 23 feet, 5½ inches, but on his first two tries he was disqualified for passing the starting line.

Jesse sets on Olympic record of 20.7 seconds in the 200-meter run during the 1936 Games.

Broad-jump winners salute during the 1936 Olympics. Behind 1st place winner Owens is Luz Long, who befriended Owens before Hitler's eyes.

Jesse had one more chance. As he rested, one of the German athletes, Luz Long, came over to him. Long was Germany's best broad jumper, the man favored to win the gold medal if Jesse failed to qualify for the finals. But Long was not thinking about a gold medal. "You should be able to qualify with your eyes closed," he told Jesse. Then he advised Jesse to draw a line a few inches in front of the regular take-off point. "Make your take-off from there," Long said. "Then you won't foul and you should jump far enough to qualify."

Jesse followed Long's advice and qualified for the finals. In the finals Jesse beat Long and won the gold medal. Jesse's winning leap was 25 feet, 5 inches, an Olympic record.

Jesse and Long became fast friends. Six years later America and Germany would be at war and Long would be fighting on the Italian front for the Germans. But nobody could ever convince Jesse that Long believed Hitler's theories of racial supremacy. Long had proven his true beliefs to Jesse in the Olympics.

Jesse's Olympic heroics did not end at the broad jump. He set another Olympic record in the 200-meter dash. Then he won his fourth gold medal by running first leg for America's world-record-breaking 400-meter relay team. Although Hitler never congratulated him, the rest of the world recognized Jesse as a hero. His track-and-field performance had been spectacular.

Jesse was cheered throughout Europe as he took part in post-Olympic track meets, then was hailed in America when he came home. He made speeches and rode in parades honoring him. Wherever he went he displayed his warm smile, his sense of humor, his wide-ranging intelligence.

In the following years, Owens appeared in sports arenas, racing against motorcycles and horses, and worked as a personnel director for the Ford Motor Company. He finally settled in Chicago, where he worked as a radio disc jockey and part-owner of a public relations firm.

Jesse had traveled almost everywhere in the world, but perhaps his most memorable trip was the one he made to Berlin in 1951. It was his first visit there since the '36 Olympics and, as writer Norman Katkov described it, Jesse put on his old Olympic suit and jogged around the stadium during a track meet while 75,000 people cheered him. Then, as Jesse ran toward the locker room, a teen-age boy stopped him.

"Will you sign your name here, Mr. Owens?" the boy said.

Jesse signed and returned the book. Suddenly he reached out his hand. "That book," he said. "May I see it again?"

He took the book from the boy and opened it. "That's a picture of Luz Long," Jesse said. "How do you come to . . ."

"My father, sir," said the boy.

Luz Long had died fighting for the German side in World War II. Jesse was touched that Long's son had come to ask for his autograph. The Olympic star and the son of his friendly German rival walked side by side down the track and out of the stadium.

Arnold Palmer

His shirttail had a habit of coming out in moments of crisis. He grimaced painfully and twisted his strong body into persuasive, agonizing postures when his shots bounced away from their targets. In his worst agonies, he looked like a rangerider who had been hit by an Apache arrow. But when his putts fell into the hole, he laughed heartily and tossed his visor or cap into the breeze, and his happiness raced like electricity through the great throngs of people who followed him. In a game known for its finesse and emotional restraint, he was a hitter. He hit the ball hard with every club on nearly every shot.

Doing all these things—laughing, groaning, twisting, hitting and certainly winning—Arnold Palmer became the most popular champion golf has ever known. People paid money to trudge after him on the fairways, and whoop for him around the greens—Arnie's Army, they were named. They assembled in larger and louder groups than either Bobby Jones or Ben Hogan had seen in their finest hours. Often as many as 30,-000 fans ringed the fairways and greens where Palmer was playing and winning.

He was, after all, one of them. Born in the mining town of Latrobe, Pennsylvania, he never forgot, despite all his success, that this was his home. Though he became the richest golfer in history, earning $400,000 per year in prize money, endorsements and investments, he and his family continued to live in Latrobe. His closest friends are still those who knew him years ago when he lived on a hamburger budget.

Palmer was unlike every great golfer who preceded him. Where Bobby Jones was boyishly correct and aristocratic, Palmer was earthy and rural. Where Hogan was cool, aloof and concentrating, Palmer was outgoing and warm. He seemed to derive strength from the knowledge that his crowds understood and loved him. He had a quick, easy smile for everyone, and a pleasant handshake for a stranger. During the moments of greatest pressure in tournaments, he might be seen chatting with members of the gallery, of his army.

Another part of his massive appeal was that he seldom played a perfect round or even a perfect hole. With the help of his bulging arms and his strong shoulders, he usually drove long and straight. But he often hit his next shot into trouble, like the average player, then somehow struggled out of it. Finally, like the hero of a Western movie, he would make an amazing last-ditch shot to survive and win.

Famous for his comebacks, Palmer was never considered out of a tournament as long as it was mathematically possible for him to win or tie. He brought off two of his most notable rallies in 1960 in the two biggest tournaments in golf. First, on a hot Sunday in April, he came down to the final two holes in the Masters needing two birdies to win. He sank a 30-foot putt for a birdie on the seventeenth hole. On the eighteenth tee, television cameras were on him, and his army lined the fairway shouting encouragement. He pounded his drive 300 yards up the hill. Then a perfect shot with his 7-iron put the ball onto the green, only eight feet from the flag. Finally, with the crowd dramatically silent, he bent over the putt with his knees together, and calmly rapped the ball into the cup for the victory.

Two months later came the U. S. Open championship at the Cherry Hills Country Club in Denver. Through the first three 18-hole rounds, Palmer was no more in contention than the man operating the hot dog concession. Between rounds, on the final day, Palmer contemplated his situation: he was in thirteenth place, seven strokes behind, with only eighteen holes more to play. He sat with two competitors, Ken Venturi and Bob Rosburg, and a couple of newspapermen, eating a sandwich and drinking iced tea.

"It's time for me to tee off," he said, rising. "Think I'll throw a 65 into them. What'll that do?"

"Nothing," replied one of the writers. "You're too far back."

Palmer grinned. "Why, that would give me a total of two-eighty. Doesn't two-eighty always win the Open?"

"Not this time," said the writer. "You're out of it."

"Maybe so," Arnold said, walking away. "But let's shoot the sixty-five and see what

happens."

The first hole at Cherry Hills was a par 4—320 yards long. The green sat low in a valley, and it was just possible for a long hitter like Palmer to drive all the way to the green if he hit the ball just right and got a good bounce over some rocks and high grass. Palmer hit his tee shot with all his strength and determination. The ball streaked toward the snow-capped Rockies in the distance and then began dropping. It glanced off the fairway and bounced miraculously onto the green. He two-putted for a birdie—and was suddenly filled with confidence.

He birdied the second, he birdied the third and then he birdied the fourth hole. Four in a row! He was four under par, and his army was dashing across the course after him like dogs after a hare. He parred the

Arnold Palmer studies the lie for an important putt.

fifth, but he sank birdie putts on the sixth and seventh holes. He completed the front nine holes in only thirty strokes. The other players were dumfounded. From nowhere, from farther behind than he had ever been before, Palmer had come back again. One by one, the leaders began to crumble under the pace Palmer was setting. Steadily he parred the holes on the last nine and he finished with the sixty-five he had predicted. He won by a single shot in the most amazing comeback in U. S. Open history.

Through 1971, Palmer had amassed more than sixty tournament victories in professional golf, far more than any of his contemporaries. He seemed well on the way to achieving a goal he had set for himself when he became a professional in 1955. "I want to win more tournaments than anyone ever," he said then. "Winning is the name of the game. The money comes second."

But the money was there—he had won a record total of $1,460,013.16 through 1971. Among the major championships, he won the Masters a record four times, the U.S. Open once, and the British Open twice. He also won the U.S. Amateur title in 1955, shortly after graduating from Wake Forest College.

Milfred "Deacon" Palmer, Arnold's father, has been the head pro at Latrobe Country Club since 1921. He gave Arnold his first set of clubs and his surest advice: "Hit it hard."

Today Palmer admits, "My dad still doesn't think I hit the ball hard enough. I keep telling him there are certain shots you just can't hit hard, but he doesn't believe it. 'Hit it hard' he says and when I don't, he frowns. Well, I guess he was more right than wrong. I've hit it hard most of the time, and it's paid off."

122

One of the most popular golfers in years, Arnie is always surrounded by a crowd. Here he tees off in the Bob Hope Classic in 1966.

Palmer sinks the deciding putt in the 1964 Masters Tournament in Augusta, Georgia.

Oscar Robertson

As they filed into the meeting room, the University of Cincinnati varsity basketball team was perplexed. What could the coach, George Smith, have to tell them a month before the season opened? As they entered, one by one, they noticed that someone was missing—the new boy, Oscar Robertson.

"Fellows," Smith said, "this is a suggestion, not an order. We are a good team, but we have a chance to be a great one and the boy who can make us great is Robertson. We can play our normal game or we can give him the ball and set up around him and let him carry us. He'll get all the glory and all the headlines, but if you do this he'll take you farther than you ever dreamed you could go."

Smith knew that in Oscar Robertson he had something special. And because the team was also learning that he was special, they agreed to do it the coach's way. George Smith was gambling on two things he knew about the new player. Oscar Robertson had the ability to become one of the outstanding players in the country, and he was amazingly unselfish.

In the three years prior to Robertson's first varsity season, the Cincinnati Bearcats won 52 games and lost 22. In the three years known as "The Years of the Big O"—after Oscar joined them—they won 79 games and lost only nine. As Smith had promised, Robertson took his teammates farther than they had ever dreamed they could go.

Robertson led the University of Cincinnati to new heights in basketball. Here he leaps over his opponent for an easy basket.

As a boy he had grown up in a tiny frame house with a tar paper roof in Indianapolis, Indiana. His family had come to Indianapolis from Tennessee when he was four years old. Soon after, his parents were divorced and Oscar's mother was left to raise her three boys by herself.

The Robertson boys soon discovered the Sennett Avenue YMCA and the game of basketball. In Indiana, basketball is the most important sport. High-school teams are the representatives of their towns or neighborhoods and basketball stars become celebrities. In many areas the sport is played all year round.

Henry and Bailey Robertson became good basketball players—too good to be bothered by their younger brother, Oscar. "When my brothers wouldn't let me play with them," Oscar remembers, "I promised myself I would get good enough so they'd have to let me play."

Each day after school Oscar would shoot

baskets by the hour until he became good enough to play with the older boys. In his freshman year in high school he stood 5 foot 8 and weighed 160 pounds. The next year he was 6 foot 2, weighed 175 pounds and was gaining a reputation. By the time Oscar was a junior he had grown to his present height of 6 foot 5 and was known throughout the state. An all-Negro high school had never won the Indiana State championship. Oscar helped Crispus Attucks High of Indianapolis win it twice—in his junior and senior years. More than forty colleges expressed interest in Robertson, who had made the high-school All-America twice. Of the forty, he chose Cincinnati because he wanted to be near home.

At Cincinnati he was a sensation while he was still a sophomore. On January 9, 1958, he arrived in New York with a 35-point scoring average. Cincinnati was to play Seton Hall before a critical and sophisticated audience at Madison Square Garden. Many would-be All-Americas have lost their reputations in the Garden, which has been the home of big-time college basketball for many years. This was the supreme test for the heralded sophomore from Cincinnati.

"Go home ya bum," Oscar heard as he stepped on the floor for pre-game practice.

"Go back to the sticks where you belong, Robertson."

"You're in the big-time now."

But by the second half, the snickers had become rousing cheers for the sheer artistry of Oscar Robertson. He rebounded, passed, dribbled and fired in long, accurate jump shots. Oscar convinced the New York skeptics of his talent by scoring 56 points, a new Garden record.

By the end of the season, Oscar had become the first sophomore to win a national scoring championship, with an average of 35.1 points per game. He later became the first player to win the scoring title in all three varsity years. And he set collegiate records with a career total of 2,973 points and a per-game average of 33.8 points.

After his senior year at Cincinnati, Oscar made the 1960 Olympic basketball team and went to Rome. He led the United States squad to the Olympic championship, preserving the United States winning streak in that event.

In the meantime, the Rochester Royals of the National Basketball Association had moved to Cincinnati. They were counting on signing Oscar as soon as he was graduated. In the two years before Oscar began to play for them, the Royals had lost $150,000. In his rookie year attendance jumped from the 58,244 total of the previous winter to a new record of 207,020. For the first time in years the Royals made a profit. Robertson, who was being paid more than $30,000 a year, was the star attraction.

He did not restrict his contribution to drawing crowds. He helped the Royals win 33 games, 14 more than the previous season; he was named Rookie of the Year; he finished first in assists with 690 (only 25 short of Bob Cousy's NBA record). Robertson led the Royals in virtually every department for the next 10 seasons and ranked among the league's all-time leaders in points, field goals, free throws, scoring average, minutes played, field goal and free throw percentage. In the category of assists, he was nearly 1,000 ahead of his nearest rival.

The one thing Robertson had never done in Cincinnati—either in college or as a professional—was play on a national championship team. All of his selections to the NBA All-Star Game (in which he was Most Valuable Player three times) and to All-

NBA teams weren't enough to match the satisfaction of winning a team title.

At the end of the 1969-70 season, however, Robertson was traded to the Milwaukee Bucks and in May of 1971 the Big O fulfilled his dream: he and the Bucks, with Kareem Abdul-Jabbar, captured the NBA crown. Big O's team was finally No. 1.

Finally on a championship team, Robertson shoots for Milwaukee over the Lakers' Jerry West.

Jackie Robinson

When it was announced in the spring of 1947 that Jackie Robinson would play that year for the Brooklyn Dodgers, many people said, "This will ruin baseball. Nobody will pay to see a black boy play."

Before 1947, Negroes had been kept out of the major leagues through a quiet agreement of club owners. When Branch Rickey, general manager of the Dodgers, announced that he intended to use Robinson, he was breaking no law. But for a while it seemed that the rest of baseball would revolt. The Philadelphia Phillies threatened to refuse to take the field against Robinson. It later turned out that they were bluffing. St. Louis Cardinal players planned a protest strike but lost their nerve when Ford Frick, president of the National League, threatened to deal severely with them.

Yet for Robinson, the hardest part of the ordeal was a pressure that no fan could see. As Carl T. Rowan, one of his biographers, later explained it in his book *Wait Till Next Year.*

Jackie Robinson talks to Dodger general manager Branch Rickey. Other Dodgers are Gil Hodges and Gene Hermanski.

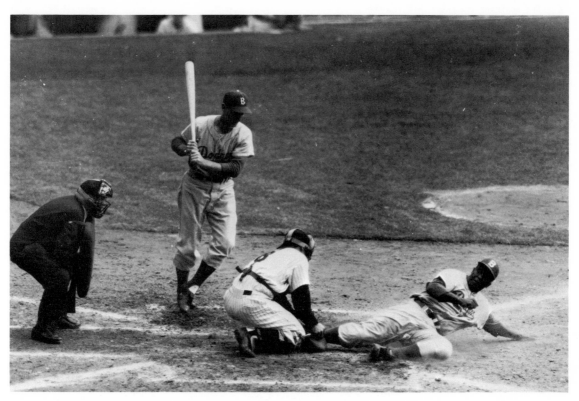

One great Robinson talent was base running. Here Jackie steals home against Yankee catcher Yogi Berra in the 1955 World Series.

How could fans sense the strain on a young ballplayer, circling the bases after Dixie Walker has hit a home run behind him, wondering whether to follow custom and stop at home plate to shake Walker's hand, or to congratulate him in the relative privacy of the dugout so as not to embarrass him by putting him in the position of having to shake hands with a Negro before thirty thousand people.

Jackie Robinson was husky and pigeon-toed. He was powerful and blazing fast. His natural style was to play the game aggressively—to get on first base and then torment the pitcher by taking a long lead and dancing back and forth on the basepath. His style was to infuriate opponents. "Hey, nigger," they would call out from dugouts, "why don't you go back to the cotton field where you belong?"

They slid into him, spikes high, and threw baseballs at his head. And yet under conditions as punishing as any that have confronted an athlete, he became National League Rookie of the Year in 1947 and went on to compile a lifetime batting average of .311. In 1962, he was elected to baseball's Hall of Fame.

The youngest of five children, Robinson was born on a small farm near Cairo, Georgia, on January 31, 1919. His sharecropper father, beaten down by poverty, deserted his family when Jackie was a small boy. Jackie's mother sold what few possessions she had and moved the family to Pasadena, California, where her brother lived. There, Jackie sold newspapers on the streets at night to help support his family and de-

127

veloped into a sensational all-around athlete.

He attended UCLA, where he became the first man in the university's history to win major letters in four sports. Intelligent and dedicated, he started a career working with underprivileged children, then served as an army lieutenant during World War II. When he returned from the army in 1945, he got a job playing baseball for the Kansas City Monarchs, a Negro club. He was twenty-six years old, no longer a young athlete.

That year Branch Rickey, general manager of the Brooklyn Dodgers, decided to break the color line in professional baseball. He dispatched a scout, Clyde Suke-

forth, to find the Negro best suited to stand up to the abuse he would receive and become a star. In August of 1945 Jackie Robinson found himself sitting in Rickey's office.

"I've investigated you thoroughly," said Rickey. "They told me out in Pasadena that you're a racial agitator. They said at UCLA that in basketball you had trouble with coaches, players and officials. I just want to tell you that my investigation convinced me that the criticisms are unjustified, that if you'd been white it would have been nothing. So I'm dismissing these rumors as not amounting to a hill of beans."

Then Rickey got down to business.

To get a regular position in Brooklyn, Jackie had to play a new position—first base. He is shown in his first major league game.

Could Robinson keep his mouth shut if ballplayers called him ugly names? Could he keep his temper when spiked?

"Mr. Rickey," Jackie said hotly, "are you looking for a Negro who is afraid to fight back?"

The rumbling timbre of Rickey's voice made his answer ring in Robinson's head: "I'm looking for a player with enough guts *not* to fight back." Jackie agreed to try.

Rickey assigned Robinson to the Dodgers' Montreal farm for the 1946 season. The Canadians acclaimed Jackie, and Montreal won the pennant in the International League. This qualified Montreal to play the Louisville Colonels, champions of the American Association, in the Little World Series. The first three games were played in Louisville and each time Robinson came out on the field the Louisville fans booed him deafeningly. Perspiring and sick at the thought that he might fail, Robinson played poorly and Montreal lost two of the first three games.

Then the series moved to Montreal. There the fans retaliated against the Kentuckians by booing the Louisville players thunderously. Jackie sparkled at bat, in the field and on the basepaths as Montreal overtook the Colonels to win the Little World Series. After the last out, when the teams had gone to their clubhouses, five thousand Canadians remained in the park, chanting, "We want Robinson! We want Robinson!"

Robinson had won his promotion to the National League, but the worst was still ahead. The public wrote him letters threatening to kill him or to kidnap his son, Jackie, Jr. In Chicago, when he slid head-first into second base, the Cub shortstop kicked him.

Yet Jackie's presence in major league baseball brought out the best, as well as the worst, in men. When he got on base against Pittsburgh, the Pirate first baseman, Hank Greenberg, would say, "Don't let them get you down, kid." When the Phillies jockeyed him mercilessly, he heard teammate Eddie Stanky shout back, "Listen, you yellow-bellied cowards, why don't you yell at someone who can answer back?"

That first season, Robinson played in 150 games, more than any other Dodger, and led the team in stolen bases and runs scored. He batted .296 and hit 12 home runs. The Dodgers won the pennant and Dixie Walker, an Alabaman, said at the end of the season that no other Dodger had done more than Jackie Robinson to keep the club in the race.

Branch Rickey's experiment was a success, but now Robinson waited for the day when Rickey would give him permission to fight back. Finally, in 1949—Robinson's third season in Brooklyn—Rickey said, "You're on your own." Robinson fought back hard. He spoke his mind and offended many who had tolerated him as long as he had remained silent. Nevertheless, he led Brooklyn to another pennant and was named the National League's Most Valuable Player.

Jackie Robinson, successful today in business and broadcasting, left baseball after the 1956 season. But by then Negro players were streaming into the big leagues. The doors Jackie had opened to ballplayers may not have been his only legacy, however. When Branch Rickey died, a television commentator said of the Rickey–Robinson story:

"Who really knows the impact this had on America? It changed a nation's way of thinking. For all we know, it might have brought on the Supreme Court's historic decision that desegregated our schools. At the least, it was far-reaching beyond the dreams of any of us."

Sugar Ray Robinson

A boy growing up in the slums of Detroit, Michigan, had two choices. He could spend his time in the streets and get an early start on a life of crime, or he could spend his time in the Brewster Center gymnasium. Walker Smith chose Brewster Center.

He was a skinny ten-year-old and he would go to the gym to watch his neighbor, a good seventeen-year-old amateur boxer named Joseph Louis Barrow. Walker would sit and watch Joseph work at the punching bags or spar a few rounds. "Someday I'm going to be a fighter like Joe," Walker thought.

When he was twelve, Walker's mother took him to live in New York City. He did not see Joseph Louis Barrow again for a long time, but he followed his career in the newspapers. Barrow now called himself Joe Louis and he had become a professional fighter. Walker boasted to the other kids about his boxing friend, who would one day become heavyweight champion of the world.

The Smiths were poor and Walker helped his mother by shining shoes and running errands. In his spare time, he went to the Salem Crescent gym in Harlem to box. George Gainford, a trainer of amateur boxers, told him he was good.

When he was fifteen, Walker tried to enter an amateur boxing tournament, but he was told he needed an Amateur Athletic Union membership card. He would not be able to get one, however, until he was sixteen. Walker was disappointed, but he was not beaten. He borrowed a card from a friend and went back to enter the tournament.

"May I see your AAU card?" asked the man at the desk. Walker handed him his friend's card.

"Ray Robinson, eh?" the man said as he wrote the name on a piece of paper. "Okay, Ray Robinson, you're in."

Walker kept the card and the name. As Ray Robinson he won the 1940 Golden Gloves lightweight championship. One night he fought in Watertown, New York. As the local sports editor watched him whip a Canadian amateur champion, he said to George Gainford, "That's a good fighter you've got there."

"Yes," said Gainford. "He's a sweet fighter. Sweet as sugar."

The next day, the name Sugar Ray Robinson was used in print for the first time. It was the name by which Walker Smith would become famous.

By the summer of 1940, Robinson had had 89 amateur fights and won them all. Gainford felt he was ready for a professional career. He matched Ray in a four-round bout at Madison Square Garden with an unknown lightweight named Joe Etcheverria and on October 4, 1940, Sugar Ray made his professional debut with a two-round knockout. Then he watched Henry Armstrong, the great, but aging welterweight champion, lose his title to a younger man in the main event.

Robinson's star was on the rise. He won his first 40 professional fights, 29 by knockouts, before losing a decision to Jake LaMotta. In 1943, there was public clamor for an Armstrong–Robinson fight—the fading ex-champion against the sensational newcomer. Ray did not want the fight, but he was persuaded to take it because a victory over Armstrong would give him an

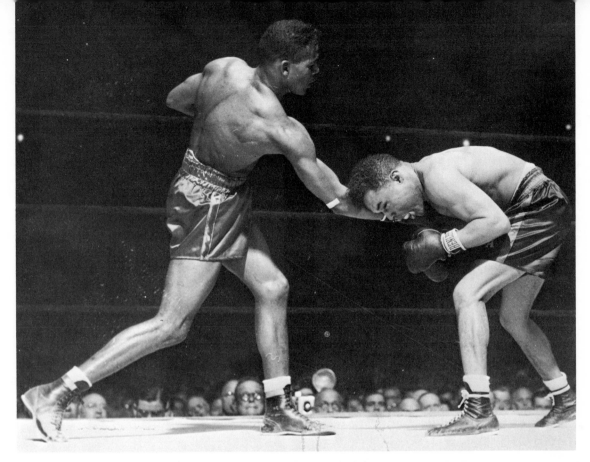

Sugar Ray scores against his boyhood idol Henry Armstrong.

early shot at the welterweight championship.

Those who saw the fight say Robinson could have knocked out Armstrong anytime after the third round. But Ray was content to win a 10-round decision over his boyhood hero. There were tears in Ray's eyes when he visited Armstrong's dressing room after the fight.

"I never would have beaten you a few years ago," he said.

"Ray," Armstrong replied, "you would have beaten me on my best night."

After the loss to LaMotta, Robinson won 34 more fights without a defeat. The press demanded that Robinson be given a championship fight. But the welterweight champion, Freddie Cochrane, refused to get into the same ring with him. Instead, he defended his title against Marty Servo, who had lost twice to Robinson, and was knocked out in four rounds.

Now Ray would get his chance. A Servo–Robinson match was made, but the champion found reasons for twice postponing the fight. The New York State Athletic Commission finally stripped Servo of his title and decreed the new welterweight champion would be the winner of a Ray Robinson–Tommy Bell fight to be held in Madison Square Garden on December 20, 1946. Robinson defeated Bell and ended a frustrating five-year chase for the title.

In his first defense of the newly acquired title, Robinson met Jimmy Doyle. Doyle had once been a first-class boxer, but he had become an erratic puncher. In the seventh round, Ray landed a thunderous right on Doyle's chin. Doyle went down, out cold. He never regained consciousness and died the next day.

Robinson was crushed. He turned over most of his prize money to Doyle's family

131

and vowed never to fight again. But friends convinced him that the death of an opponent is one of the risks every fighter takes. The memory of Doyle remained, but Ray was soon back in the ring.

He successfully defended his title four more times and when he had exhausted the supply of welterweight contenders, Ray went after bigger game. He defeated all the top middleweight contenders and was the uncrowned middleweight king. But once again he could not get a championship fight.

The middleweight champion was Jake LaMotta. He and Robinson had fought five times. LaMotta had been the only man to defeat Sugar in 123 fights, but Robinson had beaten him four times out of five. The championship match was finally planned for

Chicago on February 14, 1951. In one of the toughest, most exciting fights in history, Robinson won the world's middleweight championship when the referee stopped the fight in the thirteenth round.

As middleweight king, Robinson became widely acclaimed as the greatest fighter pound-for-pound in boxing. He moved like a ballet dancer and he hit like a sledge hammer. He was clever and fast and he had great courage in the ring. He proved his courage by doing what no other fighter had ever done. He lost his title and won it back four times.

On June 25, 1952, Sugar Ray tried for a third world championship against light heavyweight champion Joey Maxim. The fight was held in Chicago during one of the

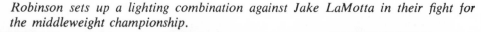

Robinson sets up a lighting combination against Jake LaMotta in their fight for the middleweight championship.

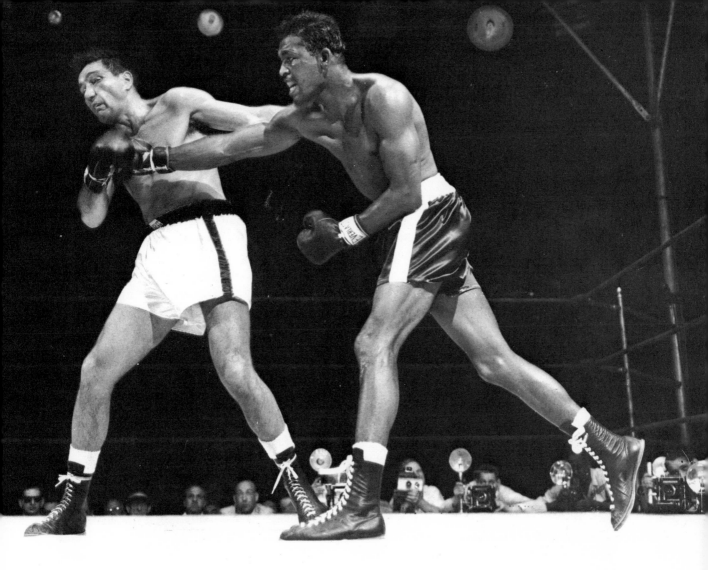

Ray staggers Joey Maxim in the light heavyweight title fight.

worst heat waves in living memory. It was 115 degrees at ringside as Robinson, 15 pounds lighter than Maxim, pounded out an early lead. In the eleventh round, the referee collapsed. In the thirteenth, Robinson swung at Maxim, spun around twice and fell to the canvas without being hit. He staggered to his corner and slumped into his stool, unable to come out for the fourteenth. Although Robinson was far ahead on points, Maxim was declared the winner and became the only man to knock out Robinson—with a big assist from the heat.

After the Maxim fight, Robinson announced his retirement. But two years later he was fighting again, despite pleas from friends to be satisfied with his remarkable career. For whatever reason, Robinson continued to fight for thirteen years after his first retirement. Finally, in 1965, at the age of forty-four he retired for good.

He quit the ring with a record of 199 fights, 173 victories, 109 knockouts, 19 defeats, 6 draws and one no-decision. He had won the welterweight and middleweight championships and had come within two rounds of winning the light-heavyweight title. Many fans still insist that no fighter has ever equaled Sugar Ray for grace, speed and all-round accomplishment.

Bill Russell

Bill Russell stood poised beneath the backboard during a semifinal game of the 1955 NCAA basketball tournament. Russell's team, the University of San Francisco, was playing the University of Colorado on the next-to-last night of the nation's biggest basketball event. One of his teammates made a shot. As the ball bounced off the rim, the 6-foot, 9¾-inch Russell sprang into action. With his back to the basket, he leaped over the Colorado defenders to grab the rebound. Then, incredibly, he jumped again and with both hands slammed the ball back over his head and down through the basket.

On the sidelines a sports writer shouted to Harry Hanin, a scout for the Globetrotters, "Did you ever see anything like that, Harry?"

Hanin shook his head in bewilderment. "No," he said, "and I never saw anything like him, either."

That was only the beginning of Russell's weekend spectacular. After defeating Colorado, San Francisco faced La Salle, the defending champions in the finals. Russell put on a show that was to force the college rulemakers to change the game. He scored 33 points as San Francisco won, 77–63. In addition, he tipped in six baskets that were credited to his teammates.

Shortly after the tournament, two rules were passed. One widened the free-throw lane to twelve feet to keep Russell, and men like him, away from the basket. No one with the ball may stay in the area between the free throw lanes for more than three seconds. The other rule made it illegal for a player to touch the ball on its downward arc toward the basket. The changes were immediately labeled "Russell's Rules." "We weren't planning to make any changes," said Dartmouth coach Alvin "Doggie" Julian, a member of the rules committee. "But after some of the coaches saw Russell's performance, they got scared." (Similar rules changes were made in professional basketball during the careers of George Mikan and Wilt Chamberlain.)

San Francisco coach, Phil Woolpert, predicted that the rules would eventually help Russell, not hurt him. "He's so much the fastest of the big men," said Woolpert, "that now he'll just leave them further behind."

Woolpert was exactly right. In 1955, Russell's senior year, he led San Francisco to an undefeated season, and a successful defense of its national title. In two seasons San Francisco had won 55 straight games. It was clear that Russell was a winner. Coach Red Auerbach of the Boston Celtics had never seen him play, but he had heard so much about him that he traded two outstanding players—Ed Macauley and Cliff Hagan—for the draft rights to Russell. Auerbach was in for a surprise when he finally did see the man for whom he had sold two of his best men. Russell was playing in an exhibition game for the 1956 Olympic team, and he had one of the worst nights of his life.

"He was terrible," Auerbach recalls. "He couldn't do anything right. I asked him over to my house for dinner after the game and the first thing he said when he came through the door was, 'I'd like to apologize for that miserable exhibition. I hope you don't think I play like that all the time.' Then I knew he'd be all right."

Russell was more than "all right." He gave the Celtics a new weapon, which was all they needed to supplement their fine team of shooters and fast-break artists. They won their first world championship in

134

Russell's rookie year. The next year Boston lost to St. Louis, and many insisted that it was because Russell was injured during the play-offs. The following year Russell was healthy, and Boston won. They won again the next year, and the year after that.

By the time Russell had played his thirteenth season, 1968-69, the Celtics had won ten championships. During five of those seasons, Russell had been named the league's Most Valuable Player. Without Bill, Boston might well have been just another ball club.

One of the amazing things about Russell's success is that he achieved it without being a great scoring threat. He has averaged only sixteen points per game with the Celtics, not a very impressive record in modern high-scoring play. "They still call

Russell accepts the Most Valuable Player award for the 1961–62 season from Maurice Podoloff (right), NBA Commissioner.

this club four shooters and Bill Russell," Bill kidded in 1961.

His greatest accomplishment has been to make defense a respectable part of the game. In his college varsity debut, he faced the University of California's Bob McKeen, an All-West-Coast player. Bill outscored his opponent, 23–14, and blocked thirteen shots, eight by McKeen. When he started playing for the Celtics, he introduced a style of defensive play that completely bewildered opponents. Instead of playing a certain man, Russell played a certain zone—daring a man to come into it. A few men in the National Basketball Association were taller, but none past or present could approach Russell's timing and instinct.

Perhaps the most amazing aspect of Russell's career is that he ever became a basketball player at all. Born on February 12, 1934, in Monroe, Louisiana, Bill was slow to develop both physically and athletically. His family moved to Oakland, California, when he was nine. Bill eventu-

Bill's defensive work is the best in basketball. He has just knocked down a shot by Dave Gambee (20).

ally attended McClymonds High School, where he was eager to do well in basketball, but as a sophomore he was only 6 feet, 2 inches tall and weighed only 128 pounds and constantly tripped over his own feet.

One day he overheard a coach complain that Bill's older brother had gone to another high school and made All-City while Bill was at McClymonds and couldn't even stand up. Bill decided that he had to prove the coach wrong. In his junior year he was third-string center and whenever McClymonds piled up a big lead, the crowd would chant derisively, "We want Russell." Bill would go in and play his heart out, although he still was clumsy and ineffective. But by the end of the season he had grown three inches and was beginning to show promise.

In his senior year he not only moved up to first-string, but he was also headed for a school scoring record. But he graduated at midterm. His total high-school career is probably the most undistinguished of any man who ever played in the NBA. Despite his lack of statistics, however, Hal de Julio, a former University of San Francisco player, noticed Bill's extraordinary sense of timing and reported on him to Phil Woolpert, the coach at San Francisco. Bill was soon enrolled at the University.

Russell grew to 6 feet 9 inches in his sophomore year and played outstanding basketball. But his team, hampered by injuries, was only fair. The next season San Francisco won its first two games and lost its third. From then on, Russell never played another losing game in college. In all seven tournaments during his junior and senior years, he was named the Most Valuable Player.

When Bill joined the Celtics, he was an immediate sensation, but he continued to develop. He worked on his shooting, and he learned to dish out as well as absorb

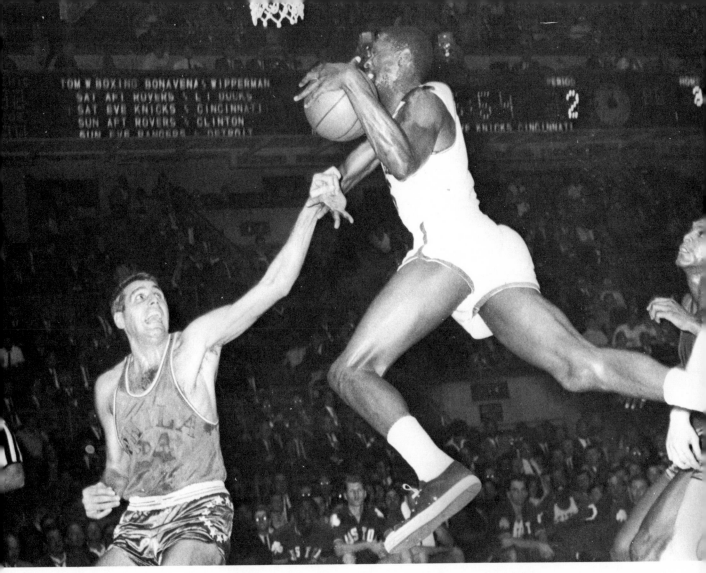

Al Bianchi of the 76ers looks terrified as Russell "zooms" in at the basket.

the bruising punishment under the basket. Intelligent and sharp-witted, Russell enjoyed the psychological part of the game, and relied on psychology to a great extent in making his defensive skills more effective. If he could prevent a player from driving on him merely by intimidating him, then he had won a battle without moving a muscle. Of course, if a player wouldn't be intimidated, Russell had other means.

When Bob Cousy retired from the Celtics after the 1963 season, Russell was named captain. He quickly demonstrated his leadership ability and filled in for coach Red

Auerbach on occasions when Red was ordered off the bench for complaining about the referees' decisions.

Although Bill insisted he never wanted to coach, Auerbach was a convincing man and in April, 1966, Auerbach announced that the Celtics' playing coach for the next season would be Bill Russell. He was the first black man to lead a major league team.

Russell retired as a coach and player in 1969 after he led Boston to still another championship. He'd won as a player; he'd won as a coach. And now he sought new worlds to conquer.

Babe Ruth

"Nice going, kid," said Jack Dunn, the owner and manager of the Baltimore Orioles of the International League. "Keep pitching like that and no one can stop you from getting into the big leagues."

Dunn was addressing a tall, dark-haired pitcher, a left-hander who had just shut out the Buffalo Bisons, 6–0, in his first professional game. His name was George Herman Ruth, and he was just getting used to a new nickname. During spring training, older members of the Orioles had been riding the 19-year-old rookie until another veteran cautioned them, "You'd better be careful. He's one of Jack Dunn's babes." From then on, the rookie was called Babe Ruth.

Getting into the big leagues in short order, Babe rapidly established himself as one of the best pitchers of his time. Brilliant as his pitching was, however, his hitting began overshadowing it early in his career. A left-handed batter, he would stand at the plate with his feet close together, stride confidently into the pitch and lash at it with a mighty swing that sent the ball soaring into the distance. The home run had been a rarity before Ruth came along. He turned it into a devastating weapon and turned himself into baseball's most famous personality.

Baltimore was Ruth's hometown. Born February 6, 1895, the son of a saloon keeper, he lived over the saloon with his family until he was seven. By then George had become more of a problem than his parents were willing to handle. He cursed, chewed tobacco, refused to go to school and ran wild in the streets.

Ruth once told sports columnist Grantland Rice about raiding his father's cash register: "I took one dollar and bought ice cream cones for all the kids on the block. When my old man asked me what I'd done, I told him. He dragged me down to the cellar and beat me with a horsewhip. I tapped that till again—just to show him he

Ruth might have been one of baseball's greatest pitchers. He is shown pitching for the Red Sox.

138

couldn't break me. Then I landed in the Home, thank God!"

The "Home" was St. Mary's Industrial School for Boys in Baltimore, a Roman Catholic protectory for orphans and neglected or delinquent boys. On his first day there, George Ruth received his introduction to baseball. A game was in progress and one team's catcher hurt his finger. George took his place. For most of the next twelve years, George lived at the Home, learning to be a shirtmaker but displaying far more interest in baseball. He came under the wing of Brother Matthias, a kindly giant of a man, who could toss a ball in the air with one hand, swing a bat at it with the other hand and knock the ball over a fence 350 feet away. George tried to pattern himself after the 6-foot 6-inch Xaverian brother, even imitating his pigeon-toed gait.

George soon became a phenomenal baseball player—a pitcher who struck out 18 to 20 opponents in seven-inning games, and then helped build up his own team's score by his batting. Jack Dunn of the Orioles signed him to a contract in 1914.

"Now, about your salary," said Dunn.

"You mean you'll *pay* me?" George asked.

"Sure," said Dunn. "Six hundred dollars a year for a starter."

If Ruth was naive in money matters, he plainly knew what to do with a baseball and a bat. By midseason he had won thirteen games for the Orioles, and his slugging had made a tremendous impression. Casey Stengel, later to become one

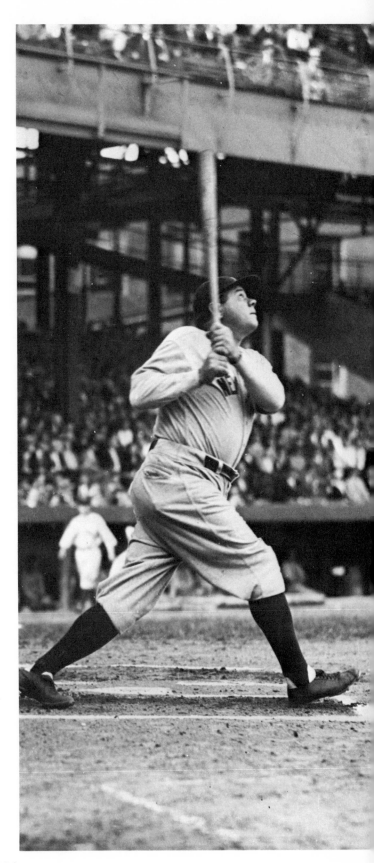

Ruth follows the flight of the ball after hitting it high and far.

139

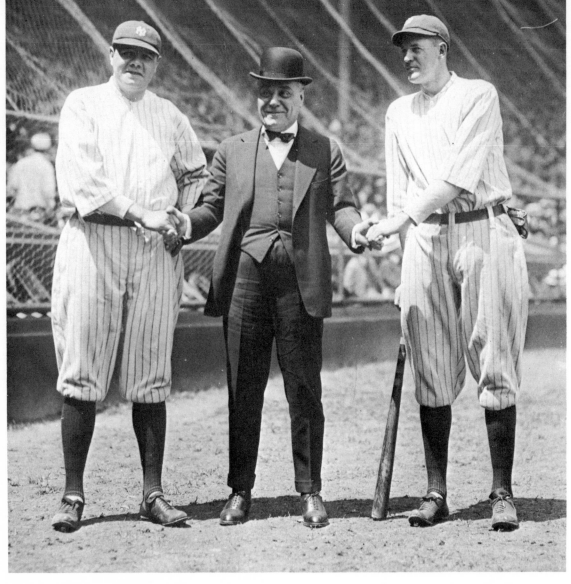

Ruth poses with another Yankee star Bob Meusel and the owner of the Yanks, Col. Jake Ruppert.

of baseball's outstanding managers, once played in an exhibition game against Baltimore. Twice, Ruth smashed the ball over Casey's head and into the stands in right field; the second blow even cleared a racing strip that encircled the park. Stengel said years later, "It was one of the longest drives I've ever seen. And remember, he was hitting a beanbag, not the lively ball we had later on."

In July, Ruth was sold to the Boston Red Sox. For the next five years, Ruth performed for the Sox, mainly as a pitcher. He won 18 games in 1915, 23 the next

year, 24 in 1917. In 1916 he beat the great Walter Johnson four times and led the league with an earned run average of 1.75.

But by 1918 Ruth was playing the outfield between pitching assignments. In 1919, his last year as a pitcher, the Babe found time to win only eight games. He was much busier and much more successful at the plate, setting a major league record with 29 home runs.

By 1918, the Red Sox were in financial trouble. In desperation they sold Ruth, who was already a national celebrity, to the

140

Yankees for $100,000 and a $350,000 loan. Together, the Babe and the Yankees launched an unforgettable era. Ruth hit 54 home runs in 1920; in 1921 he smacked 59; in 1927 he pounded out his historic 60 homers.

Off the field, Ruth lived uproariously, often enjoying himself until long after the team curfew and eating whatever he pleased in huge quantities. He was often fined by the Yankee management for breaking training rules. But despite his other concerns, he was never too important or too busy to visit a sick child.

On the field, there was no one like him. His broad shoulders and barrel chest were supported by comparatively slender legs that made him look like a ballerina. He swung his huge 54-ounce bat so gracefully that, even when he missed, the sight was a joy to behold. More often than not, though, he connected.

In 22 years in the majors, his batting average was a resounding .342. He topped .370 six times and reached .393 in 1923, his first year in Yankee Stadium, "The House That Ruth Built." Naturally the Babe christened the new park with a home run on opening day. He led the Yankees to their first seven pennants as the key man on a succession of powerful teams, the greatest of them known as "Murderers' Row" in 1927.

Ruth's salary climbed to $80,000, more than any ballplayer had earned up to that time. As someone pointed out when he signed for that sum in the depression year of 1931, it was also more than the President of the United States was making. The Babe took that in stride, saying of Herbert Hoover: "I had a better year than he had."

To the end, Ruth retained his punch. In May of 1935, he was vice president, assistant manager and occasional right fielder for the Boston Braves. One day in Pittsburgh, he walloped three home runs in one game. The last of them was the first ever to clear the right-field roof at Forbes Field. It was also the last home run that Babe Ruth ever hit. He was forty years old.

Ruth died in 1948, leaving behind a magic name and a list of records—headed by his staggering total of 714 home runs, not counting the fifteen he hit in World Series games. One of those became the most memorable of all homers. Batting against Charlie Root of the Chicago Cubs at Wrigley Field in 1932, Ruth pointed toward the center-field bleachers and proceeded to blast the ball out of the park at that very spot. Whether he actually meant to call his shot has been debated ever since, but the Babe blithely made that claim.

After the game, a sports writer asked, "Babe, what if you hadn't connected?"

Ruth seemed surprised. "Gee," he replied, "I never thought of that."

Ruth retired in 1936. He was still a national celebrity and baseball's biggest star.

Don Schollander

For the first time in his life, nineteen-year-old Don Schollander was being booed and hissed. He stood on the deck of the Harvard pool in his blue Yale sweatclothes and the partisan collegiate fans were letting him have it. Five months earlier, in the 1964 Olympics, Don had been America's greatest hero. He had been the first swimmer ever to win four gold medals in a single Olympics. But all that scarcely mattered now. He was being asked to prove himself once more.

Earlier in this freshman meet against Harvard he had won two middle-distance free-style events in record time, yet he was being hissed because he wasn't scheduled to race Harvard star Bill Shrout at fifty yards. If Don was looking for excuses to ignore the boos, he had plenty. He had just spent three months on the international banquet circuit and was twelve pounds overweight. He had been at Yale only a month and the pressure of his studies had cut his swimming workouts to a minimum. Schollander's pride, however, prevented him from seeking alibis. There was only one way for Don to silence his critics: he would face Shrout in the anchor leg of the 400-yard relay.

The cheers of the crowd built to a roar as the first three relay legs were swum. Schollander stood poised on the starting block—arms back, knees flexed. Shrout's teammate had already touched the side of the pool and Shrout was off. Then Don's teammate touched in and Don propelled himself, bulletlike, into the water. Methodically he churned out the same strokes he had worked on endlessly for the past dozen years. He was beginning to catch Shrout,

Schollander was a great hero in Tokyo during the 1964 Olympics. Swimming is a Japanese national sport.

but the 100-yard leg was almost over. Summoning his last ounce of reserve, Schollander suddenly drew even with just a few feet remaining. He stretched out his fingers as though they were being pulled by invisible wires and, finally, touched the tile wall. He had beaten Shrout by a mere inch or two.

As an exhausted Schollander sat in the water, his big chest heaving, the Harvard fans stood and gave him a long, heartfelt ovation. They had come to the meet expecting to see the world's best swimmer and they hadn't been disappointed after all. It had been only a freshman swimming meet, but Don had learned long ago how important it was to meet even the slightest challenge.

Born on April 30, 1946, to Martha and

142

Wendell Schollander, Don got his first real lesson in fortitude when he was eleven. For two years he had dominated the age-group swimming program in his hometown of Lake Oswego, Oregon, setting numerous national records. Then pneumonia struck. Don was in bed for a month and when he recovered he wanted to quit swimming entirely. During his illness, he had moved into a higher age group and, when he returned to the pool, he couldn't beat the bigger boys.

Don's father, however, didn't want his son to take the easy way out. "You can quit swimming if you want to," his father told Don, "but it will be when you're at the top of your age group, not at the bottom."

Don suffered setback after setback in the next two years. His big problem was that he just wasn't growing. A couple of times a week he would stand back-to-back with his mother in front of a full-length mirror to see if he had passed her in height. She

stood all of five feet. Finally, when he was thirteen, Don began to shoot up and his swimming kept pace. By the next year he was back on top of his age group, had set eleven national records and was beating college boys in the Northwest.

Wendell Schollander had vowed that, if he ever had a son with athletic ability, he would give him every chance to reach the top. He decided that if Don were to succeed he would need top coaching and competition, and for that, he would have to leave home. At first Mrs. Schollander was hard to convince, even though she herself had been an outstanding swimmer. After his mother had been convinced, Don had to be shown that his success as a swimmer depended on top coaching that couldn't be obtained at home.

"It was a hard decision to make," says Don. "I didn't like the idea of leaving my friends and I just plain didn't like the idea of leaving home. But here I had been working hard for six years and I just

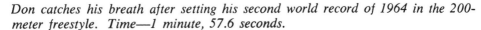

Don catches his breath after setting his second world record of 1964 in the 200-meter freestyle. Time—1 minute, 57.6 seconds.

couldn't throw all that away. Swimming was that important to me."

Don finally decided to move to Santa Clara, California, because of the fine reputation of its swim club, run by George Haines. He moved there in January, 1962, and his progress was spectacular. At the outdoor AAU championships that year, Don, still only sixteen years old, equaled the world record in the 200-meter free-style for his first national men's victory. From then on he was nearly invincible, holding or sharing world records in as many as three events at one time.

When it came time for the 1964 Olympics, Schollander was fully developed—at 5 feet 11 inches, 175 pounds—and fully prepared to put on a show that never had been seen before. He became the dominant swimmer on a team that dominated the Tokyo Games. He won his first gold medal at 100 meters with an Olympic-record time of 53.4 seconds, coming from behind in the last five meters. He set a world record of 4:12.2 at 400 meters and helped set two more in the 400- and 800-meter free-style relays.

The Japanese have the same reverence for championship swimmers that Americans have for World Series heroes. Wherever Don went in Japan, a crowd was sure to

follow. His impact on the rest of the world was nearly as great. For months after the Olympics, letters and gifts continued to pour in to the Schollander home. On one December day in 1964, Don's mother counted 98 letters and cards. There was a music box from a Yugoslav sports writer, lollipops from a Japanese girl and a film of one of Don's races from, of all people, a Harvard man, Class of 1916.

People were attracted not only by Don's swimming victories but also by his winning personality. He had the poise of a grown man but still kept his clean-cut youthfulness. He was sought by universities with outstanding swimming programs: Indiana, Michigan, Harvard, Yale, Southern California. But he insisted that swimming was only a minor consideration compared with his desire to be a doctor. After much thought, he finally chose Yale. "What I like about it," he said, "is that I'm there on a partial academic scholarship based on need. That means if I don't want to swim a stroke, I don't have to."

The freedom of choice meant a lot to Don, but once he arrived at Yale he knew it would be impossible to stay away from the pool. In many respects he had everything to lose and nothing to gain by continuing to compete. He had already reached the pinnacle of swimming, and where could he go from there except down?

But Don kept swimming. He led Yale in intercollegiate competition and in 1968 he won two more Olympic medals—a gold and a silver—in Mexico City. Afterward, he retired from competition to accept challenges out of the pool.

At the 1964 Olympics Don collected a gold medal for the 100-meter freestyle.

Jim Thorpe

The railroad station was jammed. Students from Lafayette College were crowding onto the train platform eagerly awaiting the arrival of the Carlisle Indian School's track and field squad. No one would have believed it a few months earlier. A school that nobody had heard of was suddenly beating big, famous colleges in track meets. Surely these Carlisle athletes would come charging off the train, one after the other, like a Marine battalion.

The train finally arrived and two young men—one big and broad, the other small and slight—stepped onto the platform.

"Where's the track team?" a Lafayette student asked.

"This is the team," replied the big fellow.

"Just the two of you?"

"Nope, just me," said the big fellow. "This little guy is the manager."

The Lafayette students shook their heads in wonder. Somebody must be playing a joke on them. If this big fellow was the whole Carlisle track team, he would be competing against an entire Lafayette squad.

He did. He ran sprints, he ran hurdles, he ran distance races. He high-jumped, he broad-jumped. He threw the javelin and the shot. Finishing first in eight events, the big fellow beat the whole Lafayette team.

The big fellow was Jim Thorpe, the greatest American athlete of modern times. He was born on May 28, 1888, in a two-room farmhouse near Prague, Oklahoma. His parents were members of the Sac and Fox Indian tribe and he was a direct

Jim was that football rarity—he could do everything with equal facility.

145

descendant of the famous warrior chief, Black Hawk.

As a Sac and Fox, Jim had the colorful Indian name Wa-Tho-Huck, which, translated, means Bright Path. But being born an Indian, his path was not so bright. Although he had the opportunity to hunt and fish with great Indian outdoorsmen, he was denied opportunity in other ways. The United States government controlled the lives of American Indians and, unlike other people, Indians did not automatically become citizens. It was almost impossible for an Indian to gain even a fair education and extremely difficult, as a result, for an Indian to rise high in life.

Young Bright Path seemed destined to spend his life in the Oklahoma farmland. But when he was in his teens, the government gave him the chance to attend the Carlisle Indian School in Pennsylvania. Soon Carlisle was racing along its own bright path to athletic prominence. In whatever sport Jim Thorpe played, he excelled. He was a star in baseball, track and field, wrestling, lacrosse, basketball and football. He was so good in football, in fact, that most other small schools refused to play Carlisle. The Indian school's football schedule soon listed such major powers of the early twentieth century as Pittsburgh, Harvard, Pennsylvania, Penn State and Army.

Thorpe was a halfback. He was six-feet, one-inch tall, weighed 185 pounds and had incredible speed and power. He built upon these natural gifts daily. He would watch a coach or player demonstrate a difficult maneuver, then he would try it himself. Inevitably, he would master the maneuver within minutes.

Thorpe was not only a fine runner, he was also a crunching blocker and tackler. And he could pass, punt and place-kick.

In 1908, he kicked three field goals to help beat powerful Penn State, 12–5. In 1911 he scored 17 points in 17 minutes against Dickinson, then led Carlisle to upset victories over Pittsburgh, Pennsylvania and Lafayette. Finally, he kicked four field goals as Carlisle beat the nation's top-ranked team, Harvard.

During every game, opponents piled on Thorpe, trampled him, kicked him and punched him, trying to put him out of action. They were never successful. Years later someone asked him if he had ever been hurt on the field. "Hurt?" Thorpe said. "How could anyone get hurt playing football?"

But Jim never played his best when he felt he would have no fun playing. "What's the fun of playing in the rain?" he once said. And his Carlisle coach, Pop Warner, once said, "There's no doubt that Jim had more talent than anybody who ever played football, but you could never tell when he felt like giving his best."

Despite occasional lapses, he usually gave his best. In 1912, he scored 198 points, including 25 touchdowns. Against heavily favored Army he carried three opponents across the goal line to score Carlisle's first touchdown, passed for the second touchdown, ran back a punt 90 yards for the third touchdown and ran back another punt 95 yards for the fourth. The little school of Indians won, 27–6.

Football, though, did not provide Thorpe with his finest hour. He was selected for the United States Olympic track team in 1912, and went to Sweden with the team for the Games. On the ship, while the other athletes limbered up, Thorpe slept in his bunk. In Sweden, while other athletes trained, Thorpe relaxed in a hammock. He never strained when he didn't feel it necessary.

146

Thorpe came out of his hammock when the Games began, to take part in the two most demanding Olympic events. He entered the pentathlon competition, a test of skill in five events: 200-meter run, 1500-meter run, broad jump, discus and javelin; and the decathlon competition, a series of ten events: 100-meter run, 400-meter run, 1500-meter run, high hurdles, broad jump, high jump, pole vault, discus, javelin and shot put. Though most athletes were utterly exhausted by the decathlon alone, Thorpe breezed through both events, his dark hair flopping, his smile flashing, his muscled body gliding along the track. He finished first in both the pentathlon and decathlon, one of the great feats in Olympic history.

"You, sir," King Gustav V of Sweden told Thorpe as he presented him with two gold medals, "are the greatest athlete in the world." And William Howard Taft, the

Winning both the pentathlon and the decathlon at the 1912 Olympics, Thorpe was the athletic wonder of the age. Here he throws the javelin.

President of the United States, said, "Jim Thorpe is the highest type of citizen."

King Gustav V was correct, but President Taft was not. Though Jim Thorpe had brought great glory to his nation, though thousands of people cheered him upon his return to the United States and attended banquets and a New York parade in his

honor, he was not a citizen. He did not become one until 1916. Even then, it took a special government ruling because he was an Indian.

Jim Thorpe was a hero after the Olympics and a sad, bewildered man not too much later. Someone discovered that two years before the Olympics he had been paid a few dollars to play semiprofessional baseball. Though many amateur athletes had played for pay under false names, Thorpe had used his own name. As a result, he was not technically an amateur when he competed at Stockholm as all Olympic athletes must be. His Olympic medals and trophies were taken away from him and given to the runners-up.

After this heartbreaking experience, Thorpe turned to professional sports. He played major league baseball for six years and did fairly well. Then he played professional football for six years with spectacular success. His last pro football season was in 1926. After that, his youthful indifference to studies and his unwillingness to think of a nonsports career caught up with him. He had trouble finding a job, and his friends deserted him. He periodically asked for, but never was given back, his Olympic prizes. From 1926 until his death in 1953, he lived a poor, lonely, unhappy life.

But in 1950 the Associated Press held a poll to determine the outstanding athlete of the half-century. Despite his loss of the Olympic gold medals and a sad decline in fortune during his later years, Thorpe was almost unanimously chosen the greatest athlete of modern times.

Thorpe also played major league baseball, but his success was limited because he couldn't hit a curve.

148

Johnny Unitas

The young man trying to hitch a ride on Highway 17 out of Olean, New York, that night in September, 1955, looked lonely and sad. His name was Johnny Unitas and he had every right to be discouraged. The Pittsburgh Steelers had just cut him from their squad in training camp. He was returning to Pittsburgh—his home town—where he had a wife, a young daughter and no job.

Twice before, the Lithuanian boy had been rejected by football teams. After high

Unitas once threw at least one TD pass in each of 47 consecutive games.

school, two great universities had told Unitas that he was too small for the sport. At 138 pounds, perhaps he was. But the University of Louisville had been willing to wait for him to fill out. And by the time he left college, he stood 6 feet tall and weighed 190 pounds.

Despite his failure with the Steelers, Johnny wasn't ready to give up. He still believed he could play pro football, and he didn't feel that the Pittsburgh team had given him a chance. From his mother, Johnny had learned that it was never good to give up too easily.

"She never got discouraged, and she taught us kids to think the same way," he later reminisced. "Mother never liked football because she was afraid I'd get hurt. Yet she taught me more about football, by explaining what it takes to get ahead, than any of my coaches—and I've played for some good ones."

Johnny's father had died less than six years after the boy was born. Relatives offered to take in the four youngsters, but Mrs. Unitas wouldn't break up her family. Instead, she learned to operate her husband's coal delivery service. At night she earned more money by cleaning offices in downtown Pittsburgh.

Johnny showed his mother's determination when he kept plugging for a football scholarship after Notre Dame and Indiana had turned him down. And after the rebuff from the Steelers, he clung grimly to a part-time football career—even though it paid only six dollars a game on the rock-littered sandlots of Pittsburgh. During the week he was earning a living on a pile driver.

When a phone call finally came from the Baltimore Colts the following February, the determined Unitas was ready. Someone had seen him playing for the Bloomfield,

New Jersey, Rams and had passed along the word to the Colts. A member of their staff recalls him at camp as "a raw rookie who could throw the ball, and who listened and learned."

When the Colts' first-string quarterback broke his knee in the fourth game of the 1956 season, rookie Unitas was ready again. During the rest of the season, he completed 55.6 percent of his passes, a record for a National Football League rookie. And by the time the Colts clashed with the New York Giants on a cold December afternoon in 1958, in an NFL championship game, Johnny Unitas, now the regular Colt quarterback, proved he was ready for greatness.

Before a roaring crowd of 64,185 in Yankee Stadium, Unitas directed the Colts to a thrilling 23–17 victory in the first sudden-death overtime game ever played in the NFL. When the regular playing period ended in a tie, the game went into an overtime period in which the first team that scored won the game. The first time the Colts got the ball, Unitas coolly maneuvered Baltimore from its own 20-yard line to the winning touchdown in thirteen plays. With the ball on the seven-yard line and goal to go, he shocked students of football by calling for a pass instead of a run—a pass that set up the winning score. "When you know what you're doing," the poised Unitas said afterward, "they're not intercepted." Clearly Unitas knew what he was doing.

Vince Lombardi, coach of the Green Bay Packers, once said of Unitas: "He is uncanny in his abilities, under the most violent pressures, to pick out the soft spot in the defense." And Unitas himself

Johnny has just taken the ball from center and has the option to hand off or fade back and pass.

150

observes confidently, "No matter how good a defense is, you can always find a weakness somewhere. You find it and start hitting it. Then when they close that up, you've got to find the next weakness."

During Unitas' first season with the Colts, coach Weeb Ewbank sent in three out of every four plays. But while leading the team to NFL titles in 1958 and 1959, the maturing Unitas convinced the coach his gambling was profitable. He was named Most Valuable Player in the title game each year. In Ewbank's last several seasons at Baltimore, he turned 80 percent of the play-calling over to Unitas. Between 1956 and 1960, Unitas passed for at least one touchdown in 47 consecutive games; the previous record had been 22.

By 1963, the rest of the Colts' offensive team had worn out. Opponents were increasingly prepared for Unitas' passes and his protection broke down. But his faking and shrewd play selection continued to keep the foes off balance. Playing for a mediocre team with a 7-7 record, he completed an amazing 237 passes, one of his finest achievements.

"I like to wait until the last possible second before I throw the ball," explains Unitas. "I may get dumped a lot more that way, but I also complete a lot more passes." Getting dumped doesn't ruffle him. At one time, foes marveled at the 195-pound Colt's apparent indestructibility. But word leaked out after one season that Unitas had played the whole year with a cracked vertebra. Another year he refused to sit out with a sprained middle finger on his throwing hand. In the 1958 showdown against the

Unitas passes to Jimmy Orr from the passing pocket formed by Tony Lorick (33) and Lennie Moore.

Giants, Unitas wore a nine-pound corset of steel and foam rubber to protect three ribs broken earlier in the season.

In 1964, Unitas' health was perfect. That year the Colts fought their way back to the top of their division. Unitas finally had a strong running game to vary his attack. The balanced Colt offense, with Unitas at the controls, seemed headed for another title playoff in 1965. Then the worst injury of Unitas' career—torn knee ligaments that required prompt surgery—forced him out of the last three games and cost the Colts

a chance for the championship. For the tenth straight season, however, he completed more than 50 per cent of his passes.

In 1967, Unitas sat out almost the entire season as his Colt teammates went on to win the NFL title, only to lose to the New York Jets in the Super Bowl. Johnny made a token appearance late in the game. In 1971 Unitas gained a measure of revenge when he led the Colts to a 16–13 win over Dallas in the Super Bowl. Thirteen years after his first championship victory, Johnny proved that he could still be a winner.

After winning the 1971 Super Bowl, Unitas has trouble in the 1971 season with the Super Bowl-bound Miami Dolphins.

Johnny Weissmuller

"I want a tryout," insisted the tall, skinny fourteen-year-old. Skeptically, the Chicago Athletic Club swimming coach pointed to the pool. "Swim the length of that and back," he ordered.

Johnny Weissmuller thrashed through the water, determined to make an impression. Unluckily he made his first impression on a vice-president of the club, who happened to be lazing in the pool. The flailing teenager bowled him over. Spluttering mad, the official scared Weissmuller out of the pool —and the club.

It was the last time anyone ever embarrassed Johnny Weissmuller in a swimming pool. Johnny filled out to become a broad-chested 195-pound man. He grew to a height of 6 feet 3 inches, and became a world-renowned hero and movie star all because of his prowess in the water.

Weissmuller was the complete swimmer, not just a specialist in one stroke or at one distance. In ten years of amateur competition, he was undefeated, and he swam every race from 50 yards to half-mile. His best-known stroke was the chest-high crawl, but no one could beat him in the backstroke, either. "I got bored," Johnny liked to say, "So I swam on my back, where I could spend more time looking around." In all, he won 52 national championship gold medals, set 51 world records and was the swimming hero of the 1924 and 1928 Olympics. In 1950 he was voted the top swimmer of the half-century.

When Johnny Weissmuller was a youngster, it would have seemed highly improbable that he would ever win such honors. Born in Winber, Pennsylvania, in 1903, Johnny was a weak, spindly-legged child.

Seventeen-year-old Weissmuller poses for the cameras after breaking an AAU record.

154

Soon he and his Austrian-immigrant parents moved to Chicago. Doctors there tried to fatten him up with vitamins, cod liver oil and yeast cakes.

"Try swimming," one doctor told him. Johnny did, in the muddy Des Plaines River in Illinois. He switched to cleaner Lake Michigan and soon became serious about the sport. When he failed to get much of a welcome at the Chicago Athletic Club, he tried the Illinois Athletic Club. The instructor there was gruff, 350-pound Bill Bachrach, coach of the U. S. swimming team for the forthcoming 1920 Olympics. "Can you last a hundred yards?" said Bachrach.

"I just get warmed up at that distance," Johnny lied. He leaped into the pool and began swimming at top speed. He had never been in a pool longer than 20 yards and at the end of 75 yards he was exhausted. "Form!" Bachrach yelled at him. "Never swim for speed—always for form! Look at you—exhausted, a mess!" Bachrach turned away in mock disgust.

Johnny was undisciplined, but Bachrach saw the potential in the boy's long-legged, flat-hipped body. "Swear that you'll work a year with me without question," said Bachrach, "and I'll take you on. You won't swim against anybody. You'll just be a slave and you'll hate my guts, but in the end you just might break every record there is."

True to his word, Bachrach put Johnny through a murderous training program. At the end of the year, the coach was ready to unveil his product. Johnny responded by winning four races and setting four national records in the AAU championships. Most of Weissmuller's opponents felt his performance had been a freak, but Johnny quickly convinced them that it wasn't. In meet after meet he was unbeatable. He topped himself in the 1923 AAU

indoor meet. Swimming the crawl, he won the 50-, 100-, 220- and 500-yard free-style titles and anchored the Illinois Athletic Club's winning half-mile relay team. Then, still not out of breath, he switched to the 150-yard backstroke and broke the world record by 6.8 seconds.

The supreme challenge awaited Johnny at Paris, France, in the 1924 Olympic Games. There he would swim for the first time against Duke Kahanamoku, the famed Hawaiian who had been the world's top swimmer. Johnny had broken all Duke's records, but many felt the Hawaiian's great experience would make the difference when the two raced side by side. Johnny's followers also were worried that he might spread himself too thin. He had won a place on both the U.S. water polo squad and the 800-meter relay team. Could he compete in both those events and still have enough left for the 100- and 400-meter individual races? Weissmuller was gambling on his undefeated record to prove that he could.

The field for the 100 meters was the strongest ever assembled. There were Arne Borg, the unbeaten "Swedish sturgeon," Katsuo Takaishi, the first of many Japanese champions, and Duke and Sam Kahanamoku. Duke's brother was almost as good as he was. There was no question about *this* race—whoever won it would be the world's best. At first Duke Kahanamoku still seemed to be the top man, just as he had been in the 1920 Olympics. He held the lead by inches as the swimmers passed the half-way point. At 75 meters Duke went into the powerful drive that had left many well-known swimmers catching the waves. But he could not shake Weissmuller. Johnny matched him stroke for stroke. Now it became a test of endurance, an asset that Johnny had in abundance. Method-

Johnny prepares for the 1924 Olympics.

ically he took the lead by a foot, then two feet and he won, finally, with an easy handslap. His time was 59 seconds flat, well under Duke's Olympic record of 1:01.4.

Weissmuller's 100-meter victory proved to be merely a brisk warm up. Swimming against Arne Borg in Borg's specialty, the 400 meters, Johnny knocked 22.6 seconds off the Olympic record. He then won his third gold medal by being the key man for the winning U. S. relay team.

Johnny continued to enjoy amateur swimming and he kept on winning and setting records. But somehow everything seemed anticlimactic after Paris. After successfully defending his Olympic titles in the 100-

meter and the 880-meter relay in the 1928 Olympics at Amsterdam, Holland, he retired from amateur swimming. He had become one of the many exciting sports personalities of the 1920s. Now he decided it was time to trade in some of that glamor for a professional career.

He became a representative for a bathing suit company, at a salary of $500 a week. But his big chance came early in 1930 when he was asked to take a screen test for the movie role of "Tarzan, King of the Jungle." Johnny refused at first but agreed to the test when he was promised he could meet Greta Garbo and have lunch with Clark Gable. Weissmuller auditioned along with 150 other men. He was amazed when he was chosen.

"What's your name?" the producer asked him.

"Johnny Weissmuller."

"It's too long," replied the producer. "It will never go on a marquee. You'll have to shorten it to Jon Weis."

"Wait a minute," said the director. "Don't you read the papers? This guy is the world's greatest swimmer."

Although the producer had never heard of Weissmuller, he took the director's word and allowed Johnny to keep his name. Turning to the writers, he said: "Put in a lot of swimming because this guy can swim."

For the next seventeen years Johnny Weissmuller did a lot of swimming before the cameras, not to mention vine-swinging, jungle-calling and crocodile-fighting. The films made a tremendous amount of money and when the producers decided to use a younger Tarzan, Johnny switched to TV and became "Jungle Jim."

Despite Weissmuller's long movie career, the luster of his swimming achievements was never tarnished. In 1965 he was the first person named to the Swimming Hall of Fame in Fort Lauderdale, Florida. And in a sport where records are broken every week, some of Johnny's marks lasted more than twenty years. His swimming style still influences swimmers today. But no matter how many imitators there are and no matter how many hundreds of times his records are broken, it is unlikely that swimming will ever see another Weissmuller. He was the total champion.

After a long career as an amateur swimmer, Weissmuller became known to movie fans as "Tarzan, King of the Jungle."

Bud Werner

Alpine ski racing is the sport of getting from the top to the bottom of a mountain like a bullet. For years it has been a major sport in the Alps in Austria, France, Switzerland, Germany and Italy. Only recently has it become recognized as such in the United States. The reason can be stated in two words: Buddy Werner.

Wallace "Bud" Werner was one of the true pioneering athletes in America. Born on a ranch just outside of Steamboat Springs in the Colorado Rockies, Buddy had his first pair of skis fastened to his feet at the age of two. He won his first actual race at the age of six. From that point on, America had an athlete who would devote his life to winning ski races.

Over a period of ten years, from 1954 through 1964, Bud Werner changed from a daring, cocky kid of seventeen to a quiet, modest veteran known in ski chalets around the world as a celebrity of Alpine racing. From Aspen, Colorado, to St. Moritz, Switzerland, Werner was America's "uncrowned champion," the only first-rate male ski racer the United States had ever produced.

When he was eight years old, Werner was the best-known personality in Steamboat Springs. For he was already a star in the small town's annual winter carnivals. He skied through barrels and was towed on skis behind a speeding horse through the main street of town while spectators lined the frosted sidewalks.

Bud was not only a top junior racer, jumper and mountain climber in high school, he was an all-around boy and athlete. Wiry, tough and agile, he played tailback on the best football team Steamboat Springs ever turned out, and was regarded as the best player in the school's history. He was also a trumpet player in the band, often appearing for concerts on skis.

But Alpine racing was Buddy's first love because he could ski from October through May. He practiced on packed trails, across the virgin ice of nearby glaciers and in the deep powder of remote hills. He would work for hours. For the first time, it seemed, America had raised a young skier in the same atmosphere and surroundings that nurtured the talented Austrians and French who had long dominated the sport.

Werner burst on the international ski scene in 1954 at the age of seventeen, when he was named at the last moment as a replacement on the U. S. national team. He promptly showed that his presence was no mistake when he became the first American to win the noted Holmenkollen downhill race in Norway against the best skiers in the world.

If the haughty Europeans thought his first victory was a fluke, they were convinced in 1955 that Werner was going to be a threat to them for a long time. In the Stowe International downhill race in Vermont, on a 3-mile plunge known as the "Nose Dive," Werner won by 5½ seconds, leaving one of Austria's best skiers, Martin Stoltz, so far behind that he could only shake his head in disbelief. It was typical of Werner's all-out, win-or-nothing style that in the Stowe race he chose a different line from the other racers, speeding at 80 miles per hour dangerously close to the trees and crowd. But his choice paid off, and he was immediately named to the U. S. Olympic team.

Werner didn't win a medal for the United States in the 1956 Olympics at Cortina, Italy. He crashed in all three races, trying to better the all-time record of Austria's famed Toni Sailer, who won three gold

medals. By 1958, however, Werner was emerging as one of the best skiers in the world. He won the combined championship in the Lauberhorn in Switzerland, skiing's equivalent to the Masters in golf. And in 1959 he won the Hannenkahm downhill at Kitzbuhel, the biggest annual race in skiing, second in importance only to winning an Olympic or World championship (FIS) medal. For the first time, America had a skier who was favored in every race in Europe.

Before the 1960 Olympics, scheduled for Squaw Valley, California, the U. S. Alpine community was bubbling with excitement and anticipation over Werner's prospects.

Austria's retired champion, Toni Sailer, predicted, "There is only one racer in the world capable of duplicating my three gold medals at Cortina, and that is Bud Werner."

It was not to be, however. Just eight weeks prior to the Olympics, Werner broke his leg working out in Aspen. He had been practicing overtime, striving for the perfect edge for his, and America's, big chance. Looking back on his hard luck later, Werner said, "It was probably the best thing that ever happened to me. It sent me back to college to get an education. Had I won at Squaw Valley, I probably would have been a big-headed ski bum the rest of my life."

Werner shoots down the slalom course in the 1960 Winter Olympics.

Competing at Cortina, Italy, Werner helps make a place for the United States in a traditionally European Sport.

But Werner did not stop racing. In a brilliant comeback, he won the Harriman Cup in 1961, placed fourth in the world championships in 1962, won the U. S. nationals in 1963, and once again made the Olympic squad in 1964, the sixth time he had been named to a national squad.

His last season was a splendid one, considering that he was twenty-eight—an old man for ski racing. He won the grand slalom at Val D'Isere in France, getting the United States off to a great start on its pre-Olympic European tour. Through his leadership and inspiration, two young Americans, Billy Kidd and Jimmy Heuga, captured the first men's Olympic medals

ever won by American skiers by placing second and third in the slalom.

Buddy led the team back home and won three championships in the Stowe Internationals, on the same mountain where he had won his first big victory ten years earlier.

His last official race was in the slalom of the U. S. nationals in Winter Park, Colorado, a week later. In one run, he beat the field by three seconds. He was the old master, showing the youngsters how it was done, as he carved his way through sixty gates. But in the other run, he crashed, pushing himself too far and too fast. "That's Bud," said United States racer Chuck Fer-

ries. "He's going out the way he always raced. Either beating us all by five seconds, or wiping out somewhere back up on the track."

But it was not Werner's last race. A few weeks later, on April 12, Buddy was sweeping down a glacier near St. Moritz in Switzerland with sixteen other skiers. He was participating in a ski fashion motion picture, his first professional venture, for a West German film company. Suddenly there was a rumble in the normally serene Swiss Alps. It grew louder. The skiers looked back and saw a giant slab of spring snow rolling toward them. *Avalanche!*

The skiers began to scatter. Some hid behind rocks. Others tumbled and stopped and wisely took their chances of digging out of the snow. Werner did what for him was a natural thing. He flashed down the mountain, racing the avalanche. "You couldn't expect Bud to miss a chance like that, could you?" said United States coach Bob Beattie.

Werner almost made it. Near the bottom, however, another slide from a different slope overtook him. His body, buried under ten feet of snow, was not uncovered until hours later. America had lost her greatest skier, but he had died the way he probably would have preferred—racing.

There is already evidence that in the years ahead the United States will produce so many good racers that one athlete will not have to carry the world-wide burden as Werner did. But they will owe their heritage to the daredevil from Steamboat Springs, who showed America how to win in a new sport.

Werner relaxes after a 1959 meet.

Byron 'Whizzer' White

It was 6:35 P.M., a time when most of the White House reporters were finishing their stories for the next day's newspapers. Unexpectedly President John F. Kennedy called them in to his office. He had an announcement to make. The President told the reporters he was nominating Byron Raymond "Whizzer" White to be an Associate Justice of the Supreme Court. The appointment was another mark of success in the career of Whizzer White, lawyer, scholar and athlete.

Twenty-four years earlier the Pittsburgh Steelers of the National Football League had also made an announcement. They had signed Whizzer White to a contract for $15,000, more than any professional football player had ever been paid for a single season since Red Grange. The Steelers had a good reason for paying White so much.

As a triple-threat back for the University of Colorado in 1937, the 6-foot 2-inch, 190-pound Whizzer had led his team through an undefeated, untied season with his running, passing and kicking. He had topped the nation in ground-gaining and in scoring, with 13 touchdowns, 19 kicks for extra points and one attempted— and successful—field goal. Teams hated to punt against Colorado. The Whizzer averaged 31 yards per return.

On January 1, 1938, Colorado faced a heavily favored Rice team in the Cotton Bowl. Rice was a tough, well-balanced team; much of Colorado's success, on the other hand, was due to one man. In the first ten minutes of the Rice–Colorado game, one man seemed to be enough. Whizzer intercepted a pass in the opening moments and ran it back for a touchdown. A few minutes later, he passed for another touchdown and kicked his second extra point. Colorado led, 14–0. Eventually Rice turned the tide and won 28–14, but White's first ten minutes provided the real highlights of the game.

Born June 8, 1917, at Fort Collins, Colorado, Whizzer White grew up in the nearby town of Wellington. "There were about 350 God-fearing souls living in town when I was growing up," he remembers. "It was a small town—a few stores, one bank, a post office, and so on." His father, a lumberman, was the mayor, but everyone in town, the Whites included, worked hard. At the age of seven, Whizzer went to work in the beet fields.

"In the spring," he says, "you did a thing called blocking and thinning, which

White's appointment to the Supreme Court puts him at the top of the legal world, just as he once was at the top of the sports world.

162

was clearing out all but one beet every few inches along the row. They didn't have machinery for that sort of thing in those days, so you had to do everything by hand. Then twice in the summer you did the hand hoeing of the weeds, and in the fall you helped with the harvest. . . . We might make a dollar a day or maybe even two."

Neither of Whizzer White's parents had finished high school, but they insisted that he take his school work seriously. His high-school class numbered only five students. Whizzer was the valedictorian. No football scholarships awaited him, for he had suffered a broken shoulder in high school and had been prevented from showing his talent. Luckily, the state university passed out one academic scholarship to the highest-ranking student in the graduating class of every high school in the state. White got the one for Wellington, and it enabled him to go on to the University of Colorado.

In his sophomore year, White's football prospects looked dim. He injured his knee and played in only two games. Although doctors recommended an operation on the knee, White refused, fearing that the operation would end his participation in athletics. He had the knee taped up every day and took precautions on the field. When tacklers bore down on him, he would bend the knee slightly to absorb the impact of the tackle more with his back and his hips. That winter he played varsity basketball and had no more trouble with the injury. Somehow the knee had mended.

He went on to win ten letters at Colorado —four in basketball, three in football and three in baseball. In addition, he waited on tables to earn pocket money and still found time for study.

Whizzer White was also a brilliant student. He received straight A's in every

Whizzer on his way to a touchdown against Rice in the 1938 Cotton Bowl.

course but two. The two low grades were B's. In his senior year, he received a Phi Beta Kappa key for his academic achievement and was offered a Rhodes Scholarship to study law at the University of Oxford in England. He was the perfect man for the Rhodes award since one of the requirements is that the recipient excel both in scholarship and in athletics.

But the Steelers had offered him $15,000 to play football that fall, so it looked as if he would have to choose either a football career or the scholarship to Oxford. Finally Whizzer's brother, who was already studying at Oxford, convinced university authorities to postpone Whizzer's enrollment until January. He was able to report to Pittsburgh to try his fortune in the National

163

Football League without jeopardizing his scholarship.

No rookie had ever led the National Football League in any department, but in 1938 Whizzer White led the league in rushing with 567 yards—while playing for a last-place team. "I liked pro ball better than the college game," he says. "In the professional league there is no such thing as a soft game. The money part of it isn't nearly as important as some people make out. When the season starts and the whistle blows, you play for the same reason you always play games. You play to win."

Whizzer skipped the 1939 season to study at Oxford, but he returned to America in 1940 and played for two years with the Detroit Lions. In his first season at Detroit, he again gained more ground than anyone in the NFL. This made him the second man ever to win the rushing title twice. But then Whizzer quit. He had other things to do.

He enrolled at the Yale Law School but soon joined the Navy since the United States had recently entered World War II. As a naval intelligence officer, he won two bronze stars. After the war, he returned to Colorado, where he soon achieved a reputation as a brilliant lawyer. As head of the national Citizens for Kennedy movement in 1960, he helped elect a President. He was appointed in 1961 to a position in the Justice Department, where he supervised antitrust cases and helped break down segregation in the South. Then, on March 31, 1962, came President Kennedy's announcement to the press:

I am delighted to announce today that Byron White, the Deputy Attorney General of the United States, has accepted appointment as Associate Justice of the Supreme Court. I have known Mr. White for over twenty years. His character, experience, and intellectual force qualify him superbly for service on the nation's highest tribunal . . . He has excelled in everything he has attempted—in his academic life, in his military service, in his career before the bar, and in the Federal Government—and I know that he will excel on the highest court in the land.

Whizzer was no longer called by his nickname. Now he was Mr. Justice White.

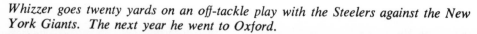

Whizzer goes twenty yards on an off-tackle play with the Steelers against the New York Giants. The next year he went to Oxford.

Ted Williams

Ted Williams squinted through the hot Florida sun at the Red Sox veterans limbering up in the outfield. He was nineteen years old and it was his first day of spring training with the Boston Red Sox. He swung around to watch a burly fellow step into the batter's cage. "That's Jimmy Foxx," whispered young infielder Bobby Doerr. "Wait till you see *him* hit." Next to Babe Ruth, Foxx was the greatest home run hitter the majors had ever seen.

According to legend, Williams replied, "Wait till Foxx sees *me* hit."

Although it was only Williams' first day in spring training, he was already sassy enough to equate himself with Jimmy Foxx. He already felt that he was the best pure hitter that baseball had ever known. As a youth and as a veteran, he would trumpet that conviction to the world. Those who still doubted him after his nineteen years with Boston had to explain a lifetime batting average of .344 and 521 home runs. In fact, Williams' average was higher than Foxx's and he had hit only 13 fewer home runs than the great slugger.

Ted became more than a super hitter. He was a larger-than-life personality, a proud, abrasive man who sometimes made the headlines by spitting at fans and warring with sports writers. Yet he also loved kids and worked to help them.

By the time he retired, Williams was almost a folk hero, but in the spring of 1938, he struck people as a loudmouthed

Just out of high school, Williams played with the San Diego Padres.

165

nuisance. He said he was a hitter and that's all he cared about. In the outfield, he paid almost no attention to catching flies. He was too busy taking imaginary swings at pitches.

Ted was sent back to the minors for one more year. Boston had a sound veteran outfield and Williams still needed experience. As he was leaving camp, the regular outfielders jeered, "So long, busher."

Ted, enraged, turned back and shouted, "I'll be back, and someday I'll be earning more dough than the three of you combined."

Williams was back in 1939. It was obvious that his long, smooth left-handed swing was the stroke of a gifted hitter. He would never swing unless his 20/20 vision told him the pitch was a strike. If it was, he would roll his supple wrists with precise timing, and the baseball would shoot from his bat with the force of rifle fire.

As a rookie, he drove in 145 runs, hit 31 homers and batted .327. He had studied hitting scientifically, and he practiced diligently. "I say Williams has hit more balls than any guy living, except maybe Ty Cobb," Williams said of himself.

Ted went into the last day of the 1941 season batting exactly .400. By sitting on the bench he could be sure of being the first man since 1930 to reach the magic number. If he played and failed to get a hit, his average would fall below .400.

"Want to sit it out?" inquired manager Cronin.

"I'll play," said Ted. "If I'm going to be a .400 hitter, I want more than my toenails on the line."

Boston was playing a double-header with Philadelphia that day. When Ted stepped up for the first time, the A's veteran catcher, Frank Hayes, looked up and said, "I wish you all the luck in the world, Ted. But you're going to have to earn it." Ted nodded, and then hit a line drive single.

Williams' smooth swing and good eyesight and lightning reflexes, made him one of baseball's best hitters.

Before he was finished, he had six hits out of eight tries, ending the season with a .406 average. No big leaguer has ever again hit .400 during a complete season. "Am I not the best hitter you ever saw?" exulted Williams after the double-header.

Many would say he was. He won six batting championships, the last one in 1958 at the age of forty. Injuries didn't stop him. He broke a collarbone during his 1954 spring training. Yet he returned to lead the league with a .345 average. He lost three weeks because of a chest cold in 1957, but still outdistanced his competitors with a .388 mark.

Perhaps his keenest disappointment was getting to play in only one World Series. That was in 1946, and he batted only .200 as Boston lost to St. Louis. But usually Williams could respond to a challenge. In his last major league at-bat, for instance, he treated his home fans to a final home run. Afterward, however, he refused to tip his cap to the wildly cheering crowd.

"I made up my mind in my second year [1940]," Ted once said, "never to tip my hat to the fans. I'll never forget that game. I struck out and followed with an error in the field. Then I heard it. They really gave it to me good. When I came into the dugout, I swore I'd never again tip my hat no matter how I was cheered."

Williams knew his shortcomings as a left fielder. "I've hurt this team with my fielding at times," he once admitted. Fans and writers rode him, too, for not being a team player. They said he didn't run out grounders and that he stubbornly refused to hit to left field when teams over-shifted their players to the right side.

After one frustrating ball game, Williams turned toward his tormentors in the stands, spat, and made an obscene gesture. Owner Tom Yawkey fined him $500. Another time Ted spat at the press box and drew a $250 fine.

Williams resented all the criticism. His rebuttals were loud and acid, particularly when addressed to the Boston press.

Yet Ted's actions, if not his words, carried a kind of nobility. He was graceful and fair on the field. And he was courageous in fighting for his country. He served a tour as a Marine pilot in World War II and he was recalled in 1952 at the age of thirty-three to fight in Korea.

He returned and hit .407 in 37 games for Boston in 1953. He played for seven more seasons and, although the Red Sox were never in contention for the pennant, Ted batted over .300 every year and kept the team in the first division. He also became the highest paid player in the game. His boast to the Boston outfielders came true—not only was he making more money than all three of them, he was making more money than some whole teams.

167

Returning to baseball as a manager, Williams smiles after his successful first season.

Baseball had always meant a lot to him. As a boy growing up in San Diego, Ted had plastered his house with pictures of his idol—Babe Ruth. He spent most of his spare time on the ball field.

The family didn't have much money. Ted's father was a wanderer, who was rarely home. And Mrs. Williams worked for the Salvation Army in order to support Ted, his brother Danny, and herself.

Ted was a pitcher for his American Legion team and for Herbert Hoover High School. Although he batted .586 and .403 in his last two years of school, San Diego of the Pacific Coast League signed him as a pitcher for $150 a month. But they soon made him an outfielder and three years later he was in the majors.

Ted never forgot what it was like as a boy to receive adult encouragement. He faithfully attends the Little League baseball championships every year in Williamsport, Pennsylvania, and over the years he has helped raise millions of dollars for the Jimmy Fund, which supports the Children's Cancer Hospital in Boston.

Williams retired in 1960 and six years later was elected to the Hall of Fame. In 1969 he came out of retirement to manage the Washington Senators (who would become the Texas Rangers in 1971) and was selected the American League Manager of the Year in his first season.

Whatever success came as a manager, though, would be overshadowed by Williams' feeling toward what he accomplished as a player. "All I want out of life," he once said, "is to walk down the street and have people point at me and say, 'There goes the greatest hitter who ever lived.' "

Index

170

173